OUTLINING
YOUR
NOVEL
MAP YOUR WAY TO SUCCESS

OUTLINING YOUR YOUR NOVEL

MAP YOUR WAY TO SUCCESS

K.M. WEILAND

PEN FOR A SWORD

SCOTTSBLUFF, NEBRASKA

Outlining Your Novel: Map Your Way to Success
Copyright © 2011
K.M. Weiland

Published by PenForASword Publishing

Printed in the United States of America.

ISBN: 978-0-9789246-2-1

Dedicated to my beloved Savior, who outlines my life much better than I do those of my characters.

And to my mother, who reads every post, watches every video, and encourages me every day.

Also by K.M. Weiland:

A Man Called Outlaw

Behold the Dawn

Conquering Writer's Block and Summoning Inspiration (Audio)

TABLE OF CONTENTS

ACKNOWLEDGMENTS

A S ALWAYS, I'M indebted to the many people who prompted, encouraged, critiqued, and assisted me throughout the writing of this book. In no particular order, those people are:

My sister Amy: #1 fan, cheerleader extraordinaire, and sharer of chocolate.

The most fantabulous beta readers on the planet: Adrie Ashford, Daniel Farnum, Lorna G. Poston, Braden Russell, Janalyn Voigt, and Linda Yezak.

My everlastingly supportive, encouraging, and opinionated family: Ted, Linda, Derek, and Jared.

My "author interviewees," ten of the wisest and most generous authors I know, all of whom consented to share their experiences in the pages of this book: Larry Brooks, Elizabeth Spann Craig, Lisa Grace, Dan L. Hays, Jody Hedlund, Carolyn Kaufman, Becky Levine, Roz Morris, John Robinson, and Aggie Villanueva.

Wordplayers everywhere: Huge shout out to the readers of my blog *Wordplay*, listeners of my podcast, and watchers of my vlog. You guys are why I do what I do. This book is for you!

INTRODUCTION

THE *ART* OF fiction is a wide-open sea of possibilities, in which the author is a wave-tossed ship along for the ride. And what a glorious ride it is! On the other hand, the *craft* of fiction puts that same ship under the expert guidance of a captain who knows how to decipher his map of those seas and then furl, trim, and jib his sails so his ship will carry him through the story on precisely the right course. Craft is all about organization, and that's where the outline—the map—becomes so important.

Through my writing blog and editing services, I've been fortunate to connect with and mentor thousands of writers. One of the topics I'm frequently asked about is outlining. How do I do it? Why do I do it? Is it worth the time and effort? My answer to the latter question is always an emphatic *yes*. Outlining has transformed my own writing process from hit-and-miss creativity to a reliable process of story craft. Outlining allows me to ride the waves of my story with utter confidence, channeling the art into the craft to produce solid stories. And the best part about outlining? It's entirely learnable.

In the following pages, you'll find an in-depth exploration of the process I've designed for my own writing. We'll take a look at the benefits of outlining and dispel some of the common misconceptions that make writers balk at the idea of outlining. We'll discover what type of outline best suits your personality, lifestyle, and writing preferences. Then we'll dive into the step-by-step process of building your outline (and, as a result, your story) from the premise up.

Because the methodology of outlining is as much about the methodology of storytelling as it is organizing your notes, we'll cover such important elements of the craft as character, setting, structure, conflict, and theme. You'll learn how to define the kind of story you want to write and how to identify and write to your specific audience. You'll also find bonus interviews with respected novelists and memoirists, who offer invaluable insights into their outlining experiences.

What you discover in the pages ahead may strengthen and expand the outlining methods you're already using, or it may transform your writing process altogether. My goal in compiling this book was to create a manual that would guide you through the basics of constructing an outline and inspire you to use this invaluable tool to take your stories to the next level.

Happy writing!

K.M. Weiland
October 2011

"In preparing for battle, I have always found that plans are useless, but planning is indispensable."
—*Dwight D. Eisenhower*

1

SHOULD YOU OUTLINE?

ENERALLY SPEAKING, WRITERS fall into two different categories: outliners and non-outliners (or, as some writers prefer it, plotters and pantsers). I say "categories," but "armies" might be a better word, since these two camps of the writing world can often be found waging passionate war for their chosen methodology. Perhaps you've encountered or even participated in a conversation like the following exchange:

> **Ollie Outliner**: I'm lost without my outline. Gotta have a road map, so I know where I'm going. It makes the journey so much easier. How can anyone write a coherent story without some idea of what's supposed to happen? Think how much time you waste writing dead-end scenes and meandering subplots!

> **Polly Pantser**: Where do you get the patience—and the time—to spend weeks, or even months, outlining a story? I'd go crazy if I had to wait that long to start writing. Besides, I lose all the sense of adventure if I know how the story is going to turn out before I start writing it.

Without question, both sides present good arguments. But how do you know which is telling the truth? Hold onto your britches—here comes the shocker.

They *both* are.

Writing—like all of art—offers few absolutes. If it did, it would quickly stultify into set patterns and tiny boxes of preconceived ideas and methods. This is nowhere more evident than in the writing process itself. It's like a deck of cards, and every writer shuffles it a little differently. Just as our stories are (we hope) distinctive, so are our personalities and lifestyles—and, as a result, our working patterns. In pursuit of bettering our craft, we voraciously study the masters by reading every how-to book and author interview we can get our hands on. But what we sometimes don't realize is, even if a particular method or routine works for one author, that singular success doesn't make it a universal principle.

In general, human beings like the protective solidity of "rules." We like the assurance that if we write one page every day, five days a week, we'll finish a book in a year and be published in two. But life doesn't work that way. Writing a page a day *may* be the perfect routine for you and allow you to finish that book in a year. But the rigidity of such a schedule might also hold you back from your ultimate productivity. You might work much better if you allowed yourself more flexibility and less pressure.

Each author must discover *for himself* what methods work best for him. Just because Margaret Atwood does X and Stephen King does Y is no reason to blindly follow suit. Read widely, learn all you can about what works for other authors, and experiment to discover which methods will offer you the best results.

My own writing routine is a continually evolving process. What worked for me five years ago isn't necessarily what works for me now, and what works for me now isn't necessarily going to work for me in another five years. With every story I write, I learn a little bit more about myself and what approaches make me most productive. I'm constantly refining my work habits, always listening to my instincts, and paying attention when I feel I'm forcing myself to observe a stricture that just isn't working.

The individual writer is the only expert of his own proficiency. Never feel as if you have to force your writing habits to mirror someone else's—no matter how successful that person may be in his own right. Find what works for you and stick with it. This is particularly true when it comes to the choice between outlining and writing by the seat of your pants. Whether you're an Ollie or a Polly may depend largely on your personality. Simple fact: Some people just don't work well with outlines. They find outlines cramp their creativity by preventing the story from evolving as they write, or they discover writing an outline scratches the creative itch to the extent they no longer have any interest in writing the book itself. But for every person who tries outlining and decides it's not for him, someone else dives in and discovers a process that transforms his writing into an efficient and organized writing machine.

I'm one of those people. I had always kept brief notes on story ideas and reminders of the direction the plot should go, but not until I began my sixth novel *Behold the Dawn* did I give outlining an honest-to-goodness go. I spent three intensive months sketching ideas and organizing scenes.

And the result?

Not only did I produce the best story I'd written up to that point, I also experienced the easiest, most exhilarating writing journey of my life. That story *flowed* as no previous story ever had, and I credit its ease almost entirely to the months I spent outlining.

After that, you would think I'd have learned my lesson. *Do yourself a favor, kiddo: OUTLINE!*

But, no, I still had to learn the hard way. I decided to jump into my next book, *Dreamlander*, without outlining. I'd spent a year researching a project that hadn't turned out, and I was feeling mentally fatigued and in no mood to do anything but *write*. The last thing I wanted to do was outline. So I steered myself off-road into the writing wilderness, sans road map. The farther I drove, the bumpier the ground became and the more I began to realize that, before I knew it, I'd be as lost as a moped driver at a Humvee convention.

I made it all of fifty pages before admitting this story was going nowhere fast. Despite characters I loved and a premise full of potential, the book was a rambling, wandering, bloated mess. After an appropriate period of pouting and oh-the-agony-ing about my plight as a writer, I finally gave in and started another outline.

Two and a half months later, I emerged with a plan of action that organized those problematic first fifty pages and offered me a clearly defined road to my destination of "The End." Never say never—but, after that experience, I will *never* begin another story without outlining. Making major adjustments in a finished manuscript of 100,000-plus words is far more painful than in a few dozen pages of outline notes.

Mostly, I outline because I'm lazy. I hate rewriting. I hate watching my burst of pride and relief at the end of a novel dissipate in the realization of a hole-riddled plot. I'd much rather know where I'm going from the beginning, rather than force my foreshadowing and plot twists into the text somewhere in my second draft. Because I'm already familiar with each pit stop along the road of my novel— thanks to my road map—it's much easier for me to visualize the big picture and realize what each scene must do to play its part.

Outlining is also a surefire antidote for writer's block. When all I have to do to discover where I'm going is look at my map, I rarely waste valuable time and brain cells staring slack-jawed at the blinking cursor.

Outlines take many forms—some of them little more than a few sentences scrawled on Post-it® Notes, some of them notebooks full of ramblings. No one says your outline has to be of any particular length. Most of my outlines fill up at least a notebook or two. A bulleted list of scenes may be all you'll need, or you may end up with *five* notebooks of scribblings. What's important is recognizing the outline as a valuable tool and then figuring out how to make it work for you.

MISCONCEPTIONS ABOUT OUTLINING

Many authors decide outlining is "not for them" after hearing the surface arguments. Before you make that decision, let's take a look at some of the common misconceptions about outlining.

Misconception #1: Outlines Require Formal Formatting

Much of the avoidance of outlining comes down to nightmarish memories of the outlines we had to learn in high school. You know the type: Roman numerals, graduated indents, and perfectly parsed grammar. Just looking at one is enough to kill your creativity:

I. The Galactic Empire attempts to squelch the Rebel Alliance.
   1. Big spaceship goes after little spaceship.
      a. Big spaceship catches little spaceship.
         i) Bad guy boards little spaceship; bad guy breathes heavily.

That's just a whole barrel of fun, isn't it? Even with an exciting story, you're more likely to snap your pencil point in frustration than wear it down to a nub with a flood of enthusiastic ideas. Formal outlines such as we learned in school may suffice for recording the bare bones of our stories. But, let's face it, they're not exactly enjoyable. By the time you reach "II. Farm boy goes on mission to save beautiful princess," you're probably going to be yawning and checking Twitter.

Fortunately, outlines don't have to look anything like this inverted staircase. In the next chapter, we'll explore a variety of outline formats, but, for now, remember outlines don't require the crossing of every T, the dotting of every I, and the buttoning of your top collar button. Rather, they should be opportunities for throwing caution to the wind, living on the edge, and breaking any rule silly enough to raise its head.

Misconception #2: Outlines Limit Creativity

Authors sometimes feel writing an outline will box them into a rigid plan, which can be deviated from only under risk of death. As soon as they put an outline on paper, they fear they've locked their story into an immutable form that can never be changed, even if they come up with a better idea halfway through the first draft.

When I was a kid, I loved those connect-the-dots puzzles. The artists would remove the lines in their sketches and replace them with spaced-out dots, each of which was accompanied by a number.

If I succeeded in connecting the dots in the correct order, I would magically end up with a kitten or a dolphin or a barn. It was fun, but it didn't allow for much creativity. If I didn't follow the dots exactly, I wouldn't end up with a picture of anything recognizable. In other words, if I didn't follow the predetermined outline, I was sunk.

Fortunately, however, this needn't be the case with a novel's outline. Like the pirate code in the movie *Pirates of the Caribbean: The Curse of the Black Pearl*, we should consider outlines to be "more like guidelines." A good outline should be a spur for creativity, not a stumbling block. The author is the master of the outline, not its slave. If and when you come up with a better idea while in the midst of writing Chapter Seventeen, by all means take a good tight hold on the muse and let its wings bear you to new and exciting shores—even if those shores weren't originally on your map.

Outlines should encourage wild creativity, daring experimentation, and focused inspiration. If you're not encountering these elements in your own outline, you're probably looking at the process in the wrong light.

Misconception #3: Outlines Rob the Joy of Discovery

Some authors rebel against outlines because they believe creating one will sap the joy of discovery they find in writing a first draft. It's true that for all the benefits outlining offers, it also requires a few sacrifices. The opportunity to write a first draft full of unexpected discoveries is one of those sacrifices. But it's not as black as it sounds. You're not *losing* the opportunity for unexpected discoveries. Not at all. What you're doing is *moving* those discoveries from the first draft to the outline. All the fun's still there; it just occupies a different place in your timeline. Thriller author and Edgar nominee Raymond Benson explains, "I figure out all the hard plot details in the outline, so you might say I really write the book when I do the outline."[1]

In many ways, an extensive outline *is* a first draft. The only difference is the outliner's process takes maybe a quarter of the time. The outline, like the first draft, is the "mistake" draft, the dry-erase board where we unveil our ideas and see how they line up on the page. Outliners and pantsers alike go through this process.

Instead of stealing creative joy, the outline expands an author's opportunities for exploring his story. He gets to experience the original act of creation in the outlining process, during which he comes up with the raw story idea, sorts out implausibilities, and fills in plot holes. In essence, he's constructing the skeleton of his story. When he later begins the first draft, he isn't retreading old ground. Instead, he's digging deeper into his understanding of his story by fleshing out the skeleton: adding the new material that will become the inner organs, skin, hair, muscles, and cartilage. Using the outline to figure out the technicalities of your plot gives you the freedom to explore your characters, settings, and themes in intimate detail in your first draft. Prolific fantasy author Jeff VanderMeer explains:

> Yes, I knew what I was going to write about in a chapter ahead of time, so there was less process of discovery in terms of what was going to *happen*. However, I found I could give more thought to *how* and *why* things happened because I already had this outline in place—on some level, I focused more on each scene, and how the scenes fit together.... I find that there's relief and a great calming effect in knowing that I can extrapolate ahead of time on the macro level, fill in a certain level of detail, and still find the writing and the actual scene-writing vibrant and exciting.[2]

Studies have proven most people are noticeably stronger in one hemisphere of the brain or the other, mostly due to their tendency to exercise one side more often. The left brain is analytical and logical, allowing us to plot our stories in a linear timeline and make rational decisions about our characters and their motives. The right side of our brains is where all the juicy creativity and raw inspiration takes place. The left brain thinks in facts; the right brain thinks in images and feelings. Neither side of the brain is better than the other. But, as writers, we can't discount the value of figuring out which side we live in most—and then stretching ourselves to explore the uncharted territories on the other side.

Utilizing an outline allows us to take advantage of both sides of our brains by divvying up the necessary responsibilities of creating a story. When we outline, the creative process can be divided into four categories: conception, outlining, writing, revising.

- **Conception** is a deeply right-brain activity. We can't explain where the first spark of an idea comes from. It's often nothing more than an image or a feeling welling up from our subconscious and demanding an explanation. My own period of conception can last several years. I allow the story to kick around in the back of my head, adding to it through subsequent flashes of inspiration, until I feel it's grown into an idea large enough to explore with my left brain.

- **Outlining** is where the left brain gets its first crack at the story. This is the phase in which I lay out all my touchy-feely ideas and analyze them with my left brain to make sure they all fit together. I identify the missing pieces and fill in the holes. Although outlines demand right-brain creativity as well, they are primarily a logical left-brain activity. I have to ask myself, *Does this character's motivation make sense? Does this event in the plot logically lead to this outcome? Does the story arc hold together?* Getting the majority of the left-brain gruntwork out of the way in the outline allows me to once again turn my creativity loose in the writing stage.

- **Writing** the story is an intensely right-brain experience. This goes against popular opinion, which believes the outline quashes any hope of creativity by imposing a predetermined plan onto the story. Just the opposite is true. Because I know where the story is going and because I've already put my left brain to work ensuring the story makes sense, I can surrender the discovery of the story details back into the capable care of my creative right brain.

- **Revising** brings the process full circle by once again imposing left-brain rationality onto the creativity of the first draft. Where the right brain has charged ahead in all its sloppy, colorful wonder, the left brain now follows behind, mopping up the excess and straightening ideas so they achieve their maximum power through clarity and cause and effect.

Misconception #4: Outlines Take Too Much Time

One of Polly Pantser's arguments against outlines is that they take "weeks, or even months" to write—and that's absolutely true. On average, each of my outlines takes me three months from start to finish. Three months is a long time—but not so long as you'll spend on the heavy-duty rewrites required to turn a rambling first draft into a tight, cohesive, salable novel.

Consider again my experience with my fantasy *Dreamlander*. Before writing my outline, I spent eight months writing fifty pages. That page count totals out at just over six pages a month. That's a page and a half a week and less than a third of a page a day.

That's pitiful.

It was also torturous. And, if that weren't bad enough, I eventually had to go back and spend an additional three months rewriting those fifty pages to bring them up to speed with the outline's improved and streamlined version of the story. I ended up spending nearly a year on a process that would probably have required only a few months had I taken the time to outline in the beginning.

Outlining requires an outlay of patience. We have to be willing to put off the actual *writing* in order to get our ducks in a row. But this preparation pays for itself in innumerable ways. A mountain climber would never consider tackling Mt. Everest without investing serious preparation time in planning his route, organizing his group, collecting and double-checking his gear, and training his body. Authors who dash off to write a 100,000-word novel are just as likely as hasty climbers to get themselves in trouble in the long run. Preparation takes time and effort, but it's always worth it in the end.

BENEFITS OF OUTLINING

So just what *do* you get when you decide to invest your time in outlining? To begin with, outlining offers all of the following benefits:

Ensures Balance and Cohesion

In an outline, you can see at a glance if the inciting event takes place too late in the story, if the middle sags, or if the climax doesn't resonate. Instead of having to diagnose and remedy these problems *after* the first draft, you can fix problems in the outline in only a few keystrokes.

Prevents Dead-End Ideas

How many times have you started writing an exciting new plot twist, only to realize—5,000 words later—that it's led you to a cul-de-sac? You either have to spend valuable time backtracking and trying to write your way around the roadblock—or you have to cut the subplot altogether and start afresh. Outlines allow you to follow plot twists and subplots to their logical end (or lack thereof) in much less time. You can identify the dead-end ideas and cull them before they become annoying and embarrassing plot holes.

Provides Foreshadowing

It's nearly impossible for an author to foreshadow an event of which he has no idea. As a pantser, when a startling plot twist occurs late in the book, you'll have to go back and sow your foreshadowing into earlier scenes. Not only is this extra work, it can often be difficult to make the new hints of what's yet to come flow effortlessly with your already constructed scenes. Because an outline gives you inside knowledge about what's going to happen in subsequent scenes, it provides you the opportunity to plant some organic foreshadowing.

Smoothes Pacing

Like foreshadowing, pacing often requires inside knowledge. If the author doesn't know the protagonist is about to be shot in the back, he can hardly adjust the pacing to introduce this shocking new event in the right manner. An outline shows you the places where your story is running too fast and the places where it is lagging and sagging.

Indicates Preferable POVs

When working with multiple points of view, it can often be challenging to know which scene should be written from which POV.

Too often, we write a scene from one character's POV, only to realize a different character's narrative perspective would probably have offered a better experience for the reader. As a result, we're forced to go back and rewrite the entire scene. Outlines allow us to make educated decisions about POV, thanks to insights regarding plot and character. Just as importantly, outlines permit us to look at the balance of our POVs over the course of the entire novel, so we can ensure each character is getting an appropriate amount of time at the mic.

Maintains Consistent Character Voice

When writing without an outline, we're often discovering the characters right along with the readers, and because our perception and understanding of our characters often evolve over the course of the story, the result can be an uneven presentation of the character's voice. Outlining—particularly if your outlining process includes the character sketches described in Chapter Seven—will help you discover your character, and his voice, before you begin portraying him in your narrative.

Offers Motivation and Assurance

Writing a novel can be overwhelming. Typing thousands of words is an undertaking in itself—but when those words all have to hang together in a way that is sensible, entertaining, and resonant, that's enough to make our knees start shaking beneath our desks. Outlines give us the assurance that we *can* craft a complete story, because, after all, there it is, right in front of us, on paper. We've *already* written the complete story; all we have to do now is fill in the blanks. And because those blanks are ones that fascinate us, outlines also motivate us to keep on writing through the tough spots, so we can get to the good stuff.

Chapter One Checklist

- ☑ Reject any misconceptions about outlining.
- ☑ Embrace the benefits of outlining.
- ☑ Open your mind to refining your writing process.
- ☑ Have fun!

ASKING THE AUTHORS

Bio: The author of *The Writing & Critique Group Survival Guide* (Writer's Digest), Becky Levine provides critique services to other writers. Visit her at beckylevine.com.

Can you describe your outlining process?

In the software program Scrivener, I create a text file/note card for each scene in the story. For every scene, I try to figure out the following: My main character's goal, the obstacles in her way (and whom they come from), what she does to battle the obstacles, if she wins or loses (usually loses), and what's at stake/what happens if (when) she loses. I'll also throw in notes about where the scene takes place, who's in it, what *their* goals and obstacles are (although I don't usually detail those as strongly), and anything else that pops into my head as I plot. I try not to start a draft until I've gone through every scene.

What is the greatest benefit of outlining?

Knowing where I'm going and knowing what matters to my main character. I have tried writing without plotting ahead; I've even tried writing scenes out of order. I flail around, and I watch my characters drift from location to location and chat about nothing. When I plot, I start to see the connections between the scenes. If I know what "should" happen next, I can make my main character actively work to get there, or— sometimes—actively work to sabotage herself. I can bring other characters into conflict with her, and I can (and this is always fun) write a great cliffhanger at the end of a chapter. Plotting ahead lets me know the bones of the story so, as I write, I can start weaving in the extra layers that make things interesting.

What is the biggest pitfall of outlining?

The biggest pitfall would be holding too tightly to the plot as a security blanket. At some point, you have to let go and write. And you have to recognize and accept you are going to come

BECKY LEVINE

to a place where your outline doesn't tell you enough—the story you've written will have detoured or morphed, and what you thought was going to happen... isn't. You can stop for a bit and do some more plotting, but you may be facing a scene you can't understand fully until you've written past it, even to the end of that draft.

Do you ever recommend "pantsing"?

The first book I worked on, I "pantsed." I never finished that book. With the work-in-progress I'm writing now, I ended up doing some pantsing toward the end of the first draft. I didn't enjoy it, and I was cranky the whole time, but it paid off. I had to push through to the end to see things clearly, and I wasn't going to be able to plot the connections, since they just weren't there. For me, I guess pantsing is a last resort. The kind of free and loose writing I hear other authors saying they love is a real struggle for me, but if you're trying to plot and just can't, go ahead and write and see what comes. It's better than sitting there day after day, staring at an empty file on your monitor and getting nowhere.

What's the most important contributing factor to a successful outlining experience?

Pushing yourself to stay the course. I like plotting, and it feels necessary as part of my writing process, but it's not easy. There are many days when I stare at my note card for a particular scene and no ideas come. My fingers are on the keyboard, but I don't have any material for them to type. This happens a lot when I get into the middle of the storyline. It's really, really tempting to skip that scene and move on to plot something farther down the line, or even just open up another file and start writing. In my experience, though, that's when the flailing starts, and I get frustrated and angry and write really awful stuff. So I grab a notebook and start doodling, or move away from my computer to stare out a window and think, or clean the house (the *seriously* last resort). I come back to the note card once I have at least a tiny sand grain of an idea. And then I keep plotting.

"Outlines help us not only to generate stories, but to organize them...."
—*Sarah Domet*[3]

2

Before You Begin Your Outline

BEFORE WE START constructing your actual outline, let's take a quick look at some important foundational elements. The outlining method described in the following chapters is the in-depth method I use in creating my own novels. You may decide to follow this method step by step, and, indeed, I encourage you to do so. I've used this method to outline five novels, and I've experienced great success with it. However, you shouldn't feel as if you *have* to follow it to the letter. If any particular part of the process doesn't feel right for you, don't hesitate to skip it or change it. After reading the rest of the book, you may decide your ideal process only requires half the steps—or you may add some new steps of your own.

Over the years, I have discovered a particular set of tools (which we'll discuss later in this chapter) that work best for my outlining process. For example, I write my outline almost entirely longhand in college-ruled notebooks. You, on the other hand, may decide to construct your outline in a Word document or on note cards or in a spreadsheet.

The only "right" way of constructing an outline is the one that offers you the most freedom for creativity. In this book, I will be presenting the methods and tools that have allowed me that freedom, but I encourage you to use what you learn about my process as a launch pad for your own experiments in creative outlining.

CHOOSING THE BEST OUTLINING METHOD FOR YOU

How do you decide which outlining method is best for you? Trial and error is your best bet. You'll never know for certain if you'll click with a particular method until you give it a try. However, you can make some educated guesses based on what you know about your personality, what has and hasn't worked for you in the past, and your own gut feelings about any particular method. For example:

• If you're short on time for whatever reason (although I caution against rushing a story unless a deadline gives you no choice), you're obviously going to need to employ a more abbreviated outlining method.

• If you're worried over-outlining may impair your creativity later on, you might want to try something as simple as jotting down scene ideas and keeping them in a file for quick reference whenever you're stuck in your first draft.

• If you're a visual learner, you might profit from a more visual representation of your outline. Instead of storing your outline notes in your computer, you might want to employ colored note cards pinned to a bulletin board—or one of the alternate options listed in the following section.

• Or, if you're ready to tackle the full-blown challenges and embrace the full-blown benefits of the total-package outlining experience, you just might want to dive headfirst into the extensive sketching and planning method explained through-out the rest of this book.

Keep in mind that your writing process will continually evolve, sometimes without your even realizing it. Different stories will require slightly (or sometimes radically) different tactics. So don't box yourself into a rigid system. Never be afraid to experiment.

Ultimately, finding the right outlining method isn't so much about choosing as it is about creating. As you read this book, grab hold of anything that strikes your fancy, give it a try, combine it with the methods you've already put into practice, and keep searching for tips you can pick up from other authors. If you're continually striving to learn about the outlining environment that allows you to work most efficiently, you'll be able to refine your writing in ways that reach far beyond the craft itself.

Different Types of Outlines

Outlines come in many shapes and sizes. Some stories may demand deviations from the standard "list" outline, in which authors compile a linear list of scenes. Linearity is often the best way to make sense of convoluted problems (and the novel is often a very convoluted problem), but sometimes it's worthwhile to use less common forms of outlining as a way of looking at a problem from a new perspective. Following are several unique types of outlines to keep in mind in addition to the more standard process explained in later chapters.

Mind Map

Mind maps are particularly valuable in looking at problems spatially instead of linearly. By writing the central theme or event at the center of your paper and surrounding it with clusters of related subjects—and those subjects with related subjects of their own—you can create an exhaustive list of possibilities for your story. Don't censor yourself. Write down any related topic that presents itself, and who knows what you may come up with. This method is particularly useful in breaking through blocks, since it taps both your subconscious and your visual mind.

Pictorial Outline

If you're a visual learner, you may find it useful to create folders of pictures related to your story. "Cast" your characters, scout likely settings, and collect pertinent props. By associating pictures with particular scenes, you not only give yourself extra details with which to flesh out the scene, you can also help yourself spot plot holes or inconsistencies. I began keeping a folder of story-related pictures while writing *Dreamlander*, and this practice has rapidly become one of the most useful (not to mention most fun) tools in my repertoire. When stuck on scenes, I will often surf the Internet for related pictures. More often than not, when I find a picture, I find my missing puzzle piece.

Map

Fantasy authors have long been known for their penchant for drawing elaborate maps of their story worlds. Often, these maps are strictly utilitarian, in that they allow writers to keep track of the various geographical features of our worlds. However, a little amateur cartography can be an integral part of world-building, even for stories grounded firmly in reality. Because a good setting is necessarily inherent to the structure of the story itself, a map can become a valuable asset in fleshing out your story. Bestselling speculative author and multiple Hugo- and Nebula-Award winner Orson Scott Card explained that drawing maps helped him refine his fantasy *Hart's Hope* in its embryonic stages. In a sketch of a walled city, he accidentally drew a gate with no entrance. Instead of erasing it, he seized upon it as an interesting idea and started asking himself questions about *why* anyone would build such a gate. He explained, "All you have to do is think of a reason why the mistake isn't a mistake at all, and you might have something fresh and wonderful."[4]

Fortunately, artistic talent isn't a requirement for an author's maps. Straight lines to indicate borders, wavy lines for oceans, and spiky triangles for mountains work just fine. When it's necessary, for whatever reason, to share my maps with my beta readers, I often recreate my intelligible-only-to-me chicken scratchings in Photoshop for a slightly more comprehensible presentation.

Perfect Review

As authors, we're never going to be completely objective about our stories. We're too emotionally involved, too attached to our characters, too excited about our plot twists, too tickled by our snarky dialogue—so much so that we can lose sight of the big picture. Often, when we begin writing a story, our ideas are hazy, and the final shape of the story is only a dim outline in the mist. The story we put on the page will never be a perfect representation of the story in our imagination, so it's little wonder we aren't always aware of where our stories fall short. But here's a little trick to narrow the gap between your idealization of your story and its printed reality: Write yourself the "perfect" review before your story ever hits paper.

If you could have a professional reviewer read your idealized concept of your finished book and totally *get it*—completely understand everything you're trying to say with your characters, plot, dialogue, and themes—what would he write about your story? Close your eyes for a moment, emotionally distance yourself from your story, and pretend you're that reviewer.

Keep the following suggestions in mind, in order to plumb the review for as much depth as possible:

- **Be specific.** Don't just let the reviewer say he loved the story. Make him tell you *why* he loved it. What parts are the best? What makes this piece really shine?

- **Be thorough.** Cover every aspect of story you can think of: plot (including arc, pacing, and originality), characters (including personalities, arc, and development), dialogue, themes, and climax.

- **Be extravagant.** Praise your story to the skies. Layer on the adjectives of adulation. After all, you're writing from the perspective of a reader who understands and loves your story just as much as you do. So have fun!

When you're finished, you'll have an explicit goal toward which you can strive in molding your story.

TOOLS OF OUTLINING

Because of the intense creative nature of outlining, I employ an entirely different set of physical tools for this part of the process than I do when actually writing the first draft.

Pen and Notebook

In the early stages of outlining, I find creative freedom by distancing myself from the temptation offered by the computer to edit and tweak before a thought is even half-formed. Returning to the caveman technology of pen and paper can have a surprisingly freeing effect on our muses. Although I write my first drafts on the computer, I've learned to free my imagination in the first rush of creation by writing my outlines longhand in a notebook. In the process, I gain a number of benefits.

Writing longhand:

• Discourages the tendency to censor or edit. Removing the temptation to glance up at a previous paragraph and switch out words and phrases with a click of the mouse allows my raw thoughts to flow onto the page. I don't judge them, I don't edit them, I don't censor them. I just pour them out.

• Brings writing down to a primal level. The tactile experience of ink on paper presents a return to writing in a purer, more instinctive form, without the intercession of complicated electronic tools.

• Provides a change of pace. When we're stumped by a tough story problem or even general burnout, changing our location and our methods can sometimes be just the trick for jump-starting our creativity.

• Frees imagination by allowing sloppiness. Something about the near illegibility of my handwriting seems to break down my need for perfection. Instead of toiling over word choice, I'm able to dash down my thoughts as quickly as they come to me. I find this particularly vital in the early creative stages.

• Frees us from distractions. Pen and paper physically remove us from the computer and all its distractions, including the siren song of the Internet.

• Allows a critical editing during transcription. The necessity of transcribing our notes onto the computer allows us the opportunity to apply a critical eye to what we've written, once the first rush of creativity is past.

- Gives us an instant hard copy. Unless your house burns down, your handwritten hard copies aren't likely to randomly self-destruct as computer files are known to do. Even if you lose your notes after you've typed them, you'll always have a hard copy as backup.

I love my technology. I love typing. I love the clean look of my Times New Roman letters appearing on the virginal white of my screen. Sometimes I even love that taunting blink of the cursor. But writing longhand is an invaluable technique that my outlining would suffer without.

Personally, I prefer college-ruled notebooks, both because their tighter lines allow more information to be crammed into the pages, and also because the confines keep my handwriting from sprawling too decadently. I use a pen, instead of a pencil, to further discourage myself from censoring or erasing my thoughts. With a fine-tipped marker, I write the year, the book's title, and the volume number of the notebook (since I inevitably fill more than one) on the cover.

yWriter Software

In years past, I used Microsoft Word to transcribe my outline notes and create my Abbreviated Outline. But then I was fortunate enough to discover yWriter. Author and programmer Simon Haynes encountered the same needs I saw in my own writing life and was able to use his programming expertise to put together one humdinger of a program. yWriter is the quintessential organizer for writers. It allows you to see your scenes, chapters, characters, and settings—among other things—all at a glance. You can keep track of such details as the date and time span of scenes, which characters are present in which scenes, which scenes take place in which locations, and which important props show up where. Plus, you can include inspirational pictures and create a nifty storyboard, showing the layout of scenes according to character POV.

Although designed as a word processor, yWriter works best for organizing my mountains of eventually undecipherable scrawl into a neat, easily accessible outline. And the great part about yWriter? It's free for the downloading from spacejock.com. yWriter is user friendly and self-explanatory for the most part, but you can find a detailed video tutorial at kmweiland.com/free.php#ywriter.

Calendar

I collect old calendars and use them to map my story's timeline. Surprisingly enough, the timeline is an oft-overlooked facet of outlining. I overlooked it myself for years, until I read about suspense author Simon Wood's misadventure:

> Nothing is worse than discovering you've written about a nine-day week (I'm talking from personal experience).[5]

When caught up in the grand whirl of plotting tragedies and travesties galore, we can easily get carried away and lose track of the time (in more ways than one). I remember, when writing my historical western *A Man Called Outlaw*, which features a dual timeline, leaning back in my chair on numerous occasions and counting on my fingers, trying to remember on which day of the week a certain event was supposed to have taken place. It could get frustrating to say the least.

Using a twelve-month calendar (banks and other businesses often provide free calendars upon request, or you can use free online services such as Google Calendar, found at google.com/calendar), I choose an appropriate month for my novel's events and start blocking out days. In most fiction, the actual dates won't matter; however, if you're writing historical fiction, which requires adherence to certain dates—and therefore agreement between dates and days of the week—it's wise to choose a calendar page that accommodates this. For example, when outlining a historical novel that began on New Year's Day, 1926 (a Friday), I took care to pick a calendar page in which the first day of the month fell upon a Friday.

In each appropriate calendar block, I scribble a brief phrase pertaining to the main event of that day. Most of my notes comprise only a word: Party; Funeral; Traveling, etc. The notes need not be extensive, since you can refer to your main outline for more details whenever necessary.

Chapter Two Checklist

- ☑ Choose the best outlining method(s) for you.
- ☑ Write the "perfect review."
- ☑ Select the outlining tools that will promote creativity and inspiration.
- ☑ Download yWriter (if you're so inclined).
- ☑ Locate a couple used calendars to track your timeline.

ASKING THE AUTHORS

Bio: The critically acclaimed and bestselling author of six psychological thrillers and the lauded writing book *Story Engineering* (Writer's Digest), Larry Brooks manages *Storyfix*, one of the leading online instructional writing sites. Visit him at storyfix.com.

Can you describe your outlining process?

I would describe my approach as the antithesis of a "make it up as you go" strategy, or "pantsing." I seek to encounter and evaluate major story points during the story development process. When I am developing a story, I work on those milestones first, in context to a Big Idea of the story itself. Sometimes I do all this story planning with flowcharts scribbled on paper, even yellow sticky notes, and finally a sequence of story moment bullets (a "beat sheet") that tell the story front to back. When viewed in a sequential context, you can tell if you've got it right, if the pacing and arc (both dramatic and character) is there, and you can fix what isn't working without having to write another draft.

What is the greatest benefit of outlining?

Creatively, it is the opportunity to explore all possible and reasonable beats or moments in a story without having to actually write it. When that happens, the writing becomes embellishment and life-giving, rather than exploration. If you know what happens—the "mission" of a scene—then writing it is one of two things: execution, or seeking a better idea. With outlining, you do that seeking pre-draft, and thus you avoid the temptation to "settle" simply because, hey, it works, I need to move on. With outlining, what simply "works" (in a drafting process) is trumped by what works best.

What is the biggest pitfall of outlining?

Whether outlining or drafting, if the writer doesn't create the story in context to a thorough understanding of dramatic structure and the principles of narrative effectiveness, it'll tank.

LARRY BROOKS

Writers who draft without this understanding are stuck between a search for these basics and a defiance of them, thinking they can make up their own structural paradigm as they go, or worse, not recognizing it exists. That said, there are no pitfalls to outlining, other than convincing yourself you can't do it or that it compromises your creative process.

Do you ever recommend "pantsing"?

I do "pants" certain scenes, but I always know the intention and mission of a scene before I write it. If you can pour a story out of your head and have the hook in the right place, put in the fore-shadowing where you need it, set up your first plot point with great anticipation and reader empathy, establish the stakes, then blow it all out of the water at the first plot point (this assumes you know precisely where that plot point goes and what it needs to do)—if you can do all that organically (because you are a prodigy or a genius or you've been doing this for decades and finally have the hang of it), then go ahead and pants. Otherwise, you're in for multiple drafts, and you're open to settling because, in not knowing this stuff, you won't recognize it when you stumble upon it.

It's all simply a search for story. You can get there planning (out-lining), and you can get there pantsing. It's just that the former is quicker and more effective, not to mention orders of magnitude more efficient.

What's the most important contributing factor to a successful outlining experience?

A solid grasp of the fundamentals, what I call the Six Core Competencies of Successful Storytelling. One of them is story structure, and this alone is the great liberator, the empowerer, of successful authors. But you need all six—concept, character, theme, structure, scene execution, and writing voice—to get into the hunt. Once you can deliver a story at this level, the bar goes up even higher, because now you need one of your six core competencies to be astoundingly good in order to stand out among a huge crowd of other writers who understand the same dramatic physics you now understand.

"…your premise is your inspiration. It's the 'lightbulb' moment when you say, 'Now that would make a terrific story'…."
—*John Truby*[6]

3
CRAFTING YOUR PREMISE

B Y THE TIME I sit down to begin outlining a story, it's usually been chasing around in my head for at least a year or two. I almost always have ideas for several main characters, a handful of scenes, a general conflict, and a broad sense of the ending. My first goal is to hammer all this down into a premise: a single sentence that conveys the plot and the theme.

Do you know what kind of story you're writing? The premise is where you discover and solidify these decisions.

> I know this sounds basic, but be able to create a mission statement along the lines of "I'm writing a relatively fast-paced action-adventure story with a subplot involving espionage and a tragic love relationship." You may vary from that description, but being able to on the macro level tell yourself what it is you're trying to do is very useful.[7]

Your premise may actually change several times throughout the outlining process, but, to begin with, it will help you focus your thoughts. Your goal is to create a sentence that conveys the characters, setting, and central conflict, first generally, as in the example in the paragraph above, and then in the most specific way possible. That's asking a lot of a single sentence, but being able to focus your story into such a compact package will help you stay on track throughout your outline and first draft.

THE "WHAT IF" QUESTION

All stories begin with a premise (a battle in space, two people falling in love, a dog getting lost), and most premises begin with a "what if" question:

- What if a little boy's brain grew too quickly for his body to keep up? (*Ender's Shadow* by Orson Scott Card)

- What if an orphan were given a fortune by an unknown benefactor? (*Great Expectations* by Charles Dickens)

- What if our dreams were actually taking place? (My own *Dreamlander*)

Every writer is familiar with the power of the "what if" question. Even when the question isn't articulated, every novel, every story, and every article is ultimately inspired by those words. Many of us, however, fail to tap the question's full potential, simply because we don't make a conscious effort to answer it.

My historical novel *Behold the Dawn*, a medieval epic set during the Third Crusade, was, in many ways, the changing point in my writing process—not in small part because it was in outlining this story that I learned to deliberately answer those magic words: *What if?*

On the first page of *Behold's* outline notebook, I wrote *What if…?*, and, below it, I dashed off every single question that popped to mind:

What if Annan (the main character) isn't a knight?

What if Mairead (the female lead) isn't nobility?

What if she doesn't die?

What if Annan kills her?

What if Marek (Annan's indentured servant) kills her?

What if she were married to Sir Enemy?*

---

*The bad guy didn't have a name at this point.

What if Annan was hired to assassinate King Richard? Prince John? The Queen?

What if Mairead were insane?

What if she were the assassin?

What if she were killed for beliefs contrary to the Church— that would maybe force Annan to reevaluate things?

What if Annan had done some indiscriminate killing as a young man?

What if he were hired by Richard to take out certain political enemies—only to be bought over and sent to kill Richard during the siege?

What if Mairead had a child by Lord William?

Most of these ideas were completely off base, some of them laughably so, and most never made it into the book. But they opened the floodgates of my imagination and prompted me to think about my story in ways I hadn't previously considered. By allowing myself to write down every idea, no matter how crazy, I came up with gems I would never have thought of otherwise.

Underneath my list of questions (which I continued to add to whenever something new popped to mind), I tried another variation of the "what if" question, by asking, *What is expected?* I made a list of everything I could conceive the average reader expecting to happen in my story—and then turned each expectation on its head to insert the unexpected wherever possible:

It's expected Annan and Mairead will fall in love. And I definitely want them to.

It's expected they'll live happily ever after. Maybe they won't— although I don't want readers to start expecting characters to die. That destroys the power of it.

It's expected the bad guy will lose and die and the good guy will win and live. Yes, I want that to happen. The ending will lack finality if Sir Enemy lives.

It's expected Annan will remain unwaveringly loyal to the Crown, to King Richard, and to the Crusade. But he doesn't care about the Crusade, and maybe he doesn't care about the King. That would be bucking tradition—to show that Richard wasn't this savior of England—he was a politician like all the rest through time.

It's expected Annan will be essentially good. But maybe he's not. Maybe he's a mindless killer. Maybe Mairead is repulsed by him. Actually, come to think of it, I like it so much better when a *good* hero is suppressed (by himself) and then rises to conquer—rather than a hero who starts out as a bad guy who changes his ways. So make Annan a good guy who just isn't, can't, or won't rise to the mark. Think Maximus from *Gladiator.*

What's unexpected?

That someone isn't who he seems.

That someone is unexpectedly alive.

That someone is unexpectedly dead. Someone is working hard to make it seem as if he is still alive.

That Lord William doesn't really die.

These simple exercises bore fruit beyond my wildest hopes. In the space of a few notebook pages, my story leapt from a simple tale of vengeance, redemption, and love in the Middle Ages, to a complicated story of intrigue and suspense.

Make the "what if" question a part of your routine for every story. Write the question out to provide yourself a solid visual, and let your imagination take off. Once you've selected the few ideas that might work, start looking for tangents: "If such and such happened, then *what if* this also happened? Or *what if* this happened instead?" The possibilities are endless.

THE PREMISE SENTENCE

"What if" questions are hugely powerful. But if we don't refine them into full-blown premise sentences, we're not taking full advantage of them. Crafting a good premise sentence is valuable for a number of reasons.

Identifies Viable Ideas

Condensing and solidifying an idea into a premise sentence gives you an immediate assessment of whether this idea will stand up for the length of an entire story. Let's take the "what if" question that inspired my fantasy *Dreamlander*: "What if our dreams were actually taking place?" It's a good idea. But we don't know if it can carry the weight of a plot until we nail down the details in a premise sentence: "Renegade journalist Chris Redston discovers his dreams are really memories of a world he lives in while he sleeps, which he will, reluctantly, have to fight to save from destruction."

Solidifies Characters, Conflict, and Plot

A premise sentence forces you to identify a main character (as explicitly as possible: you'll note my premise sentence indicates his name, his occupation, and a personality trait), a central conflict, and, as a result, a general plot. Your "what if" question gives you an idea; your premise sentence gives you a story.

Distills the Book's Essence

In the madcap frenzy of creation, particularly in the early days of inspiration, it's easy to be overwhelmed with all the colorful possibilities. A story has so many potential directions that the task of selecting the best one can prove difficult. Sometimes you'll be chapters into the story before realizing you should have taken another path. A premise sentence is like a mini-outline, one that's useful even to those who dislike outlining. Writing down your idea (and it is important to actually write it down) gives you a guiding star by which to direct the frigate of your story.

Guides You to the Next Question

Once the premise sentence has given you the central crux of your story, the next step usually becomes obvious. As soon as I knew my premise for *Dreamlander*, I knew some of the questions that needed to be answered. What was this dream world like? Why was Chris the only one who discovered it? Why was it in danger of destruction?

Provides an Easy Answer to Questions About Your Story

When well-meaning friends, family, and fans ask, "So what's your new story about?", you hem and haw, flustered by the difficulties of explaining a 300-page novel in a few words. The easy solution is to offer them your premise sentence. It's an answer that satisfies their curiosity and allows you to appear confident and prepared.

Prepares You for Selling Your Work

Finally, creating a premise sentence early in your writing process prepares you for pitching your work to agents, who inevitably require a concise, gripping description of your story. If you start now, you can polish it to perfection by the time you're ready to start shopping your book.

PRE-OUTLINE QUESTIONS

How many times have you been thrilled by a book's amazing plot idea—only to be disappointed because the author never took full advantage of the idea's capabilities? It's relatively easy to come up with a plot idea, set the characters in motion, and then watch hopelessly (or sometimes obliviously) as the story meanders away from the original premise idea.

Inevitably, new and improved ideas will present themselves to you as you dig deeper into your outline, your first draft, and your multiple edits. But if you can grab some of the best ideas while your story is still nothing but a premise, you can save yourself the work of having to revamp the story in time-intensive ways later on. Stop for a moment at this stage and ask yourself if you've taken full advantage of the possibilities offered by your premise. Your premise is the foundation for every other facet of your story—character, setting, theme, plot. Without a solid premise, your story will turn into the Leaning Tower of Pisa, no matter how strong the other elements may be.

Enchantment, Orson Scott Card's modern take on the Sleeping Beauty legend, offers a marvelous example of how to strengthen your story by taking full advantage of the premise. Card's story dumps a young man from modern America into a 9th-century Russia rife with interesting story possibilities and all kinds of conflict. Card could easily have written an entertaining tale set entirely within this framework. But because he understood his premise of magical time travel supported more, he masterfully upped the ante and turned the tables on characters and readers alike by sending the hero and his Russian princess *back* to the modern world halfway through the book. Because Card realized his premise could handle so much more than just the obvious first step of sending the hero to Russia and letting him fight his way through an antagonistic medieval society, Card offered a story that literally gave us the best of both worlds.

Take a long, hard look at your premise: Are you milking it for everything it's worth? Don't settle for the obvious or easy answers. If you have a brilliant premise, don't let a drop of that potential go to waste. For example, Card might have asked himself, "If the magic time-travel bridge can take my hero to the 9th century, why can't it also take the Russian princess back to modern America?" The purpose of these questions is to force yourself to think outside the box. Very few story ideas are entirely original. Sleeping Beauty spin-offs have been done before. *Enchantment* could easily have fallen into familiar patterns, but because Card forced himself to think outside the box, his story offered a new slant on a familiar premise.

In addition to questions specific to your premise, ask some general questions:

- What are four or five big moments that will occur in the plot?

- Can you think of at least two complications for each of these moments?

- Will these complications push your characters in ways that make them uncomfortable?

- What additional settings will these complications demand?

- Which character will be the protagonist?

- Which character will be affected most by the inciting event?

- Does this character have at least two major problems or anxieties in his life? Which offers the most potential for conflict and drama?

- How does this problem affect other characters?

None of these questions has a "right" answer. Keep evaluating your responses, looking for those that offer meaty possibilities, until you feel you've exhausted the angles for the time being. Take note, though: this isn't the end of your creating. This is just the beginning. A "well thought out [novel] ....does not include knowing in advance every line of dialogue, every scene, every exciting turning point."[8]

HOW TO BRAINSTORM

Some methods of brainstorming are more likely than others to put us in the way of viable ideas. Mind maps and "what if" questions, as well as writing prompts and free writing, are all valuable methods because they all have one thing in common: they allow us to move past the critical, analytical side of our brains and get in touch with the "dream zone" in the back. This kind of brainstorming is what Robert Olen Butler refers to as "dreamstorming."[9]

Our work (and our lives) would be pretty useless without the logical sides of our brains. Our writing would be a frenetic wash of color and emotion indistinguishable to anyone but ourselves. We need the logical side of our brains to help us organize our thoughts into coherency. But the power of art is usually the result of the right side of our brains—the unconscious side. How do we keep our conscious brain out of the way long enough to tap into our unconscious creativity?

- **Make time to dream.** Quietude can be difficult to find in the midst of our hectic lives, but even just a few minutes of daydreaming every day can reap significant results.

- **Don't censor yourself.** Creativity is a delicate and temperamental flower that often wilts under the weight of "the rules" or the hot carping breath of our infernal internal editors. Not everything that bubbles up from the depths of your unconscious creativity will have worth, but give yourself time to get it on paper and let it rest before judging it.

• **Tell your left brain to zip it for a while.** Your left brain can be a pushy character. When he's telling you he thinks he knows best how to write this story, tell him to stow it for a bit, so his chatter doesn't distract you from the offerings of your right brain. Your left brain will get his chance later.

• **Focus on the senses.** Our subconscious works on a level deeper than words. It feeds our brains with images, sounds, smells, tastes, and feelings, which our conscious brains then translate into words. Nothing wrong with those words (they're the tools of our trade, after all), but give a try to focusing on the raw sensations. Close your eyes and visualize the scene you're writing. What colors stand out? What can you smell? What does your body feel like? This is the best way I know to find those all-important "telling" details that bring a scene to life.

• **Listen to your gut instinct.** Ever get that itchy feeling that something is wrong with a story? You're cruising right along, having a good ol' time with your characters… but something just doesn't feel right. I've learned to trust my gut instinct. I can't think of an instance in which it has ever failed me. The only trick is learning to interpret what it's saying.

Most authors would be the first to admit the best of their writing is beyond even them. It comes from someplace outside the conscious realm. Once we recognize and accept that fact, we are then able to take advantage of the tremendous opportunity of harnessing our unconscious minds. The two sides of our creativity—the conscious and the unconscious—working in harmony, the one pulsing and pounding ahead, the other slowing and refining, are capable of fantastic things.

Chapter Three Checklist

- ☑ Write down your story's primary "what if" question.
- ☑ Craft your premise sentence to
  - identify your story's central idea
  - solidify your character(s), conflict, and plot
  - distill the book's focus (romance, mystery, historical, etc.)
- ☑ Answer the appropriate pre-outline questions to make sure you're considering all the options your premise offers.

ASKING THE AUTHORS

Bio: The author of three cozy mystery novels, Elizabeth Spann Craig hosts the blog *Mystery Writing Is Murder*, twice listed as one of *Writer's Digest's* 101 Best Websites for Writers. Visit her at mysterywritingismurder. blogspot.com.

Can you describe your outlining process?

I usually prefer writing a book without using an outline. But, currently, I have an editor who requires an outline before I start work on the first draft. So outlining is something I've learned to adapt to.

First, I come up with a quick summary of the book I plan on writing—almost like back cover copy. That gives me a focal point for the book. With my outlines, I hit all the plot highlights. I'll introduce the main characters as they come "onstage," introduce the suspects through their interactions with the intended victim, then continue on to the discovery of the first body, and the investigation following the discovery (questioning each suspect). Then there's a second body discovered, and the investigation commences again before the sleuth solves the case and confronts the killer.

My goal for the outline is simply for my editor to see the bones of my book—and for her to hopefully say, "This sounds like a good story."

Basically, I'm just treating the outline as if someone were asking me, "And *then* what happened?" I'm hitting the book's main events and not going into a lot of detail—but enough to explain character motivation, show some character growth, and touch on any important subplots.

What is the greatest benefit of outlining?

I found that, although the outlining process is time-consuming, it made the actual writing of the book go more smoothly afterwards. Also, knowing the main plot was planned meant I

ELIZABETH SPANN CRAIG

could devote more time to subplots and descriptions during the first draft—those are usually elements I add during later drafts.

What is the biggest pitfall of outlining?

I think the biggest pitfall of outlining is the feeling we're doing something a little clinical and less creative. I try to approach the outline as a brainstorming process—as "what iffing" on paper. Once I infused the process with some creativity, it went a lot smoother for me.

Do you recommend "pantsing" for certain situations and outlining for others?

I think if you're getting *stuck* when you're following your outline, give yourself permission to stray a little. Ask yourself if the story would change for the better if you took a different approach to the scene. Also, I think it's easier to be really vague about a particularly emotional scene in an outline... referring to a frightening or upsetting scene in the more clinical format of an outline can make it difficult to really put yourself into the frame of mind needed to write the scene when you're writing the first draft.

What's the most important contributing factor to a successful outlining experience?

For me, it was the moment when I relaxed a little and realized I could edit the outline. I told myself the outline, like a first draft, was not going to be the perfect plan for the book until I tweaked it. I gave myself permission to take some wrong turns and to just treat the exercise as brainstorming on paper. By the time I turn in the final draft of the outline, it's just the way I want it... but it takes some rewrites to get there.

"Enter the writing process with a childlike sense of wonder and discovery. Let it surprise you."
— *Charles Ghigna*[10]

4

General Sketches, Pt. 1:
Connecting the Dots

OW THAT YOU'VE crafted your premise into a secure sailing vessel, you can embark into the deeper waters of your story by writing what I call "General Sketches." You'll be logging the ideas you've already formed, harpooning for plot holes, and testing the cut of your story arc. General Sketches are outlining in its broadest manifestation. You won't be plotting every detail of your novel just yet. Right now, you're slitting the packing tape and opening the box that holds your story. You'll be discovering the beautiful and disparate parts inside that box and learning how they fit together.

In many ways, this is the most important stage of the outline, since it's where you give yourself permission to throw every idea—no matter how offbeat—onto the page. You'll be writing down what you already know about the story, crafting it into a synopsis of sorts, and discovering the plot holes. Take the time to ask yourself lots of "what ifs" and "whys." Why is the character behaving this way? Why is she bitter about her past? What if he makes a radically different decision at a crucial point in the plot?

The few scenes of which you're already aware are the dots in your connect-the-dots puzzle. Now, it's time for you to figure out how and why the lines follow this particular pattern. Thanks to the outlining process, that job is much more easily accomplished, since you can concentrate all your attention on answering the questions, rather than also struggling to construct full-blown scenes, complete with characters, dialogue, and a consistent plot.

THE SCENE LIST

After the initial spark of inspiration, most of my stories require several years of "brewing" before they tell me they're ready to be put onto paper. Booker Prize-winner Margaret Atwood pointed out that "you know when you're *not* ready; you may be wrong about being ready, but you're rarely wrong about being not ready."[11] As soon as you get the green light from your muse, start by listing the scenes you already have in your head.

Summarize Your Scenes

In *Behold the Dawn*, I opened my General Sketches with the question, "So what do I know about this story?" and then spent the next dozen pages summarizing, in linear order, everything I knew would happen to my characters:

> Marcus Annan, a disillusioned professional soldier, is wounded during the Third Crusade and captured by Saracens. He is nursed back to health by a Scotswoman who had accompanied her doomed husband to the War and was herself captured by the Muslims.
>
> Annan, once recovered, is given the opportunity to escape. Feeling a debt of gratitude to the Lady Mairead, he offers to aid her escape. For some important reason, they marry, with the intention of separating once in France or England.
>
> They escape and are met by Annan's indentured servant Peregrine Marek. They keep their marriage a secret from him.
>
> Annan has an enemy, for some reason. Can't remember his name, so we'll just call him Sir Enemy. They are at odds over something. (Etc.)

Some of the events you write down may actually end up happening *before* the beginning of your book, but, at this point in the outline, you shouldn't worry about shaping the format of the story or choosing the best place to begin the first chapter. Right now, you're just getting all your thoughts on paper.

List Your Scenes

In *Dreamlander*, I took a slightly different approach by writing down the main events in a list format:

1. Chris dreams of a woman who warns him to stay in his world and then shoots him.

2. Chris receives strange letters warning him to "stay away from the shrink."

3. Chris learns he visits a parallel world when he sleeps.

4. Chris wakes up in Lael in the middle of a battle.

And so on. The important thing isn't to create new scenes or try to fill in the blanks in the plot. All you need to do at this stage is dig through your imagination (or perhaps even your physical notes, if you're given to scribbling ideas on napkins and scraps of paper) for every single idea you've ever come up with in relation to this story. Not all of them will work; some will be downright silly. But because all of them were conceived more or less organically and have had time to grow to maturity in the warmth of your imagination, every single one is worth writing down.

Highlight the Problem Areas

When you reach a part of the story that doesn't make sense or needs to be fleshed out, write yourself a quick note and move on. My General Sketches are littered with comments such as "and then I'm not sure what happens" and "this part is all pretty sketchy in my mind." These blank areas are the secret tunnels that will lead us to adventures unknown when we start digging into them. For example, in the first paragraph of my General Sketches from

Behold the Dawn, I underlined every idea I knew would need to be fleshed out:

> Marcus Annan, a disillusioned professional soldier, is wounded during the Third Crusade and captured by Saracens. <u>He is nursed back to health</u> by a Scotswoman who had accompanied her doomed husband to the War and was herself <u>captured by the Muslims.</u>
>
> Annan, once recovered, is given <u>the opportunity</u> to escape. Feeling a debt of gratitude to the Lady Mairead, he offers to aid her escape. <u>For some important reason, they marry</u>, with the intention of separating once in France or England.
>
> They escape and are met by Annan's indentured servant <u>Peregrine Marek</u>. They keep their marriage a secret from him.
>
> <u>Annan has an enemy, for some reason.</u> Can't remember his name, so we'll just call him Sir Enemy. They are at odds over something.

At the end of each day's outlining session, I go back over the pages I've written and make a note in the top margin, indicating what kind of information is found on each page (e.g. "Sketches," "Character Sketches: Marcus Annan," "Outline," etc.) so I can easily find what I'm looking for later on. Then, armed with highlighters, I run back over my notes for the day and mark in orange anything that needs further work. Later, when I actually begin my outline, I'll mark in blue any idea that's solid and complete enough to be transcribed. Whenever I come up with an idea that belongs either earlier or later in the outline, I'll mark it in pink with an accompanying arrow, indicating where I'll need to move it when I'm ready to start transcribing.

Because writing longhand precludes the use of Word's Find feature and because riffling through a notebook full of sloppy handwriting can make locating a specific idea only slightly less daunting than deciphering Morse code, taking a few minutes at the end of each writing session to highlight pertinent portions saves a lot of time and frustration in the long run.

CONNECTING THE DOTS

Your basic scene plan may be pages long (as it was for me in *Behold the Dawn*) or just a few paragraphs (as it was in *Dreamlander*). Length isn't important. All that matters is you now have a working map of your story so you can see at a glance what's missing. In other words, you can see the dots outlining the picture that will become your story, and you can see the blank spots between those dots, representing the plot holes in your story.

At the end of *Behold the Dawn*'s scene list, my next step was to acknowledge the many questions still needing to be answered. From there, I dove right in with the most salient questions (Who was Annan's enemy? And why?) and started experimenting with possible answers, some of which raised additional questions:

> Maybe Annan's enemy is a bishop or something. (I'll have to be careful with that though. He has to be a completely fictional character. Can't taint a historical character with my own views or plot needs.)

> Could Annan have a secret in his past?

> Maybe he's a runaway monk.

> Whoa, now there's a thought. If I did that, it would mean Annan's indifference toward life is only a pretense. He could have left the Church because of indifference, of course, but that's too dispassionate for his character.

> He could have left because he saw through the hypocrisy of the Church. But I don't want to go too far against the mores of the day. Martin Luther hasn't rocked the boat yet. We can't have Annan making too many waves of his own.

> No, better, I think that he left because he was hurt—maybe a friend was killed unjustly by the bishop.

Free Write

I encourage you to forget as many of the rules of good prose as possible. Write as quickly as you can and don't stop to censor yourself.

I talk to myself on paper, sometimes in first-person, sometimes in second-person, sometimes in plurality. Anyone brave enough to decipher my notes would probably decide I was dissociative! I tell myself jokes (and allow myself to laugh at them). I gush about my characters. I use exclamation points with abandon. The point is: Release your inhibitions and just write. Let yourself meander down side trails, explore dusty nooks and crannies, and dream wild dreams. Only a small portion of these ramblings will be of use in the final draft. But the only way to find the treasure is to get yourself all mucky crawling around in the jungle. No prim and proper tea here, ladies and gentlemen. It's time to don your pith helmet and embark on a safari.

Listen to Your Body

As much as we want readers to intellectually appreciate our writing, we need them, even more, to react with utter, unthinking emotion to the underlying pull of the story and its characters. The magic ingredient in fiction is that special something that socks readers right in the gut and leaves them breathless with joy or sorrow (or maybe wabi-sabi, the Japanese term for that impossibly beautiful combination of the two). We have to be careful we don't let the (very important) intellectual side of the craft take precedence over the even more important guidance of our primal, instinctive, emotional gut feelings. Our emotional and physical responses to our ideas are often the most accurate indication of their value.

We've all read books that were perfectly executed, but somehow lacked that magic. I thoroughly enjoyed the magnificent word craft of Diane Setterfield's *The Thirteenth Tale*, but, for whatever reason, it never connected with me emotionally. On the other hand, Jane Porter's perhaps technically (and certainly historically) suspect *The Scottish Chiefs* never fails to wring me out like a washrag after dinner dishes. A story that connects with me emotionally will win my approval, even if it fails on certain structural levels. I'll forgive your plot issues if you make me love your characters and resonate with your themes. When you can connect with the mysterious, often unpredictable realm of readers' emotions, you're likely to hook them into not only reading your story, but also carrying it with them for the rest of their lives.

How do you create emotionally resonant stories? It's simple: Create stories with which *you* resonate. Learn to listen to your body and identify emotional connections and reactions. Whenever I hit on an idea that makes me literally gasp, that makes my lungs "collapse," I know I've got something. Even if my body were to let me, that's not a feeling I can afford to ignore. When a story or a character or a theme rips at my heart or fills me with joy, I know I've tapped a powerful emotion, and, if I can channel that emotion, then I'll likely give readers a similar experience. Bestselling mystery author Elizabeth George spoke about how writing is as much a physical experience as an intellectual one. The "committee in your mind,"[12] as she calls it, can lead you astray, but your gut reactions are rarely wrong. National Book Award finalist Dan Chaon explains it as:

> …a little minnow-flash of unshakable emotion—a character, a situation, a voice…. You know you've got it when you feel a little tingle in your chest, a flip-flop of your stomach.[13]

In her children's novel *Emily of New Moon*, L.M. Montgomery referred to the feeling as "the flash," which kept the main character "a-thrill and expectant."[14]

Whenever my chest collapses, when I can't breathe, when my stomach seems to be practicing aerial dives, *that's* when I know I've hit an idea that matters. Even if it should end up mattering to no one else, it matters to me. And, during the creative stages, that's more than enough.

Will all readers react to your story in the same way you do? Probably not, because not everyone is emotionally stimulated by the same things. Ultimately, emotional reaction—that heart of all stories—is subjective. What resonates with me won't necessarily resonate with you. But the starting place for any powerful story must be the author himself. If a story doesn't resonate first and foremost with you, why believe it will ever be able to touch a reader?

What does *your* physical response to emotional resonance feel like? If you don't already know, you need to find out.

Ask Questions

When you get stuck—and you *will* get stuck—remember to ask yourself questions. Instead of stating the problem—"the princess is trapped in the high tower"—phrase it as a question—"how can I get the princess out of the high tower?" It's amazing how much creativity can be unleashed with a question mark. For a squiggly line with a dot at the end, it wields untold power. Periods put a full stop on inspiration. They indicate whatever idea the preceding sentence holds is complete unto itself and doesn't require further exploration. A question mark, on the other hand, is a swinging door, urging us to step forward and peek through the opening. What's in there? How can we find it? How can we use it?

In *Dreamlander*, I used explicit questions (and implicit questions via the word "maybe") to explore a character I felt I wasn't using to her full capacity:

> How can I involve Allara a little bit more? Utilize her viewpoint more? She can't just stand around talking to the Garowai all day—she has to have something to *do*.
>
> What does a princess do exactly? Hmm.
>
> What does a Searcher do?
>
> Well, she rides her great black stallion around—talks to the Garowai—encourages her people—visits the Dream Lake— spurns courtiers, etc. I think I'm going to kind of have to play her by ear. Unless… she was reacting (vs. acting). Once she's found Chris, her essential job is done, so the fact that she's the Searcher really doesn't have much bearing.
>
> But could it?
>
> What could the Searcher do—beyond find Chris?
>
> Obviously, she's got a good rapport with the Garowai.

Maybe the only person allowed to speak with the Garowai is the Searcher. So she's kind of a go-between for Lael and the Garowai. But that still has her just standing around talking to him.

Maybe she has some project to help in the Lake Country's defense (or the defense of Ori Réon). I don't want her to be all female warrior, but I don't want her to be a damsel in distress either. Maybe she rides to the various cities and settlements, recruiting soldiers and warning the people? She would take her bodyguard along, of course (except when he's busy training Chris).

I think Tireus's army needs to be drawn up against Mactalde's even before Chris crosses the worlds. No safe and secluded castles—I want dangerous battlegrounds, thank you very much. So Allara can be very involved in her father's war effort.

Few skills are inherent to the writing life. Most are learned along the way, as they become necessary. But the one absolutely necessary trait is an unabated sense of curiosity. Curiosity may have killed the cat, but it's the life's blood of a writer. Even when you think you have a plot problem all figured out, push a little farther by asking a few more questions. What if something *else* happened in this scene? What would change as a result? Would the resultant shifts be for the better or the worse?

As we've already discussed, one of the reasons outlining is so valuable is because it gives us the opportunity to explore every possibility in sight, with minimum effort and words expended. In writing a first draft, it might require weeks and thousands of words to experiment with a different slant on a scene. An outline takes only minutes and a couple dozen words to follow a scene to its logical end and figure out whether or not an idea will work.

Checklist for Chapter Four

- ☑ Summarize or list all the scenes you're aware of.
- ☑ Use a highlighter to mark any area in need of further development.

☑ Fill in the blanks between scenes (connect the dots) by asking questions.

☑ Free write, ignoring spelling and grammar mistakes.

☑ Identify your physical reaction to good and bad ideas.

☑ Ask questions (instead of making statements) whenever you're stumped.

ASKING THE AUTHORS

Bio: The author of *Nail Your Novel*, Roz Morris is a bestselling ghostwriter and an editor for a top London literary consultancy. Visit her at nailyour novel.com.

Can you describe your outlining process?

First, I write my ideas for the story on index cards and shuffle them about to get them in the most dramatic order. This means I don't have to make decisions about where I'm going to put an event or a revelation until I have seen the whole story and how every element works together. I make lists of what I need to research—which will give me more ideas for story events or characters. I also might write a detailed synopsis to allow me to experiment with some of my themes and make the story richer.

What is the greatest benefit of outlining?

Planning before I start writing means I can engineer the story so it has maximum impact and explores my themes in the way I want. I can choose the best place to introduce a twist or plant a clue, and build the tension. A lot of the power of a story is in its structure—what characters do and what that means to other characters—rather than the moment by-moment details and the language. So I establish the framework, and then when I write the text I can concentrate on enjoying the words. I find doing it this way makes for a much more satisfying story—and I enjoy the writing more.

What is the biggest pitfall of outlining?

Some writers feel outlining can make you stale with a story. But a first draft is usually very rough. Even if you have labored to make each sentence beautiful, you usually need to go back and polish the dialogue, structure, pace, descriptions, and so on. You might go through the manuscript as many as ten times, in detail—and after that, questions of spontaneity seem rather laughable.

ROZ MORRIS

However, it's worth keeping your very first draft. The first time you write a scene may be rough, but it will also be fresh. Sometimes if you feel you've worn the story out or polished too far, go back and look at the words you used when it was unfolding on the page the first time. You often find it contains an energy you may have forgotten.

Do you recommend "pantsing" for certain situations and outlining for others?

I did once write without an outline. I got fired up by a setting and an inciting incident. I got a flash of inspiration about the characters I would throw in. I couldn't contain myself, so I started writing. I threw in more and more ideas, some good and some dreadful. But the biggest problem was I didn't have any clear idea where I was going, so eventually I ground to a halt. And by that time I hated it because trying to think of new stuff was such a chore.

However, I wouldn't say I'd never write without an outline. If I had a strong idea of the story in my head I might set sail and write a proper draft without any outline. It might work if you're writing a novel with a clear and obvious structure—for instance a journey. But that is still, in a way, following a plan. I think most writers need guidance of some kind because once we start writing we get too creative and keep inventing new things. An outline helps keep that creativity within boundaries—and you end up with a slicker, more dynamic story.

What's the most important contributing factor to a successful outlining experience?

Prepare beforehand. To write an outline, I need to already have a sense of my characters, the story's geographic setting and some ideas of key scenes. Outlining for me is joining the dots between these points, inventing what needs to go in the holes between the ideas I already have, and checking which order the events will be most powerful in. I can't do that if I'm inventing it all from scratch as I go because then I'm worrying about generating material instead of assessing how to use it. So I need to know my story in a vague sort of way before I start outlining.

"Good writing is: A combination of risk and craft."
—V. Joshua Adams[15]

5

General Sketches, Pt. 2: Key Story Factors

A S YOUR OUTLINE begins to take shape, it's important to keep in mind several key factors: motive, desire, goal, conflict, and theme. The earlier you can identify these things and ensure your plot is capable of properly incorporating them, the easier your job will be in the long run. Every so often, take a mental step back from the creative whirlwind you're scribbling onto the page and evaluate these elements. Sometimes these things can be easy to overlook as you're summarizing your plot, but the last thing you want to do is spend months on your outline only to start writing your first draft and discover you're missing a key element. I've been there, and I can tell you nothing is more frustrating or demoralizing. Take a little extra time in the early stages to make sure all the building blocks are there.

Motive, Desire, and Goal

As people, we're often judged by what we do. To a large extent, we *are* what we do. However, because others' perceptions of our actions don't penetrate to the reasons *behind* our actions, we're often judged incorrectly, or even unjustly. Our characters are no different. In a book, as much as in life, a person's actions are crucial. Readers want to understand this person by seeing what he does. Often, however, it's what a character *wants to do* that matters even more. Humans aren't always able to act upon their good or bad intentions, but does that make those intentions any less powerful—or any less defining? And, even when we do act upon them, our actions can be misconstrued by others. What we intend for good may be viewed as evil by others; what we do with selfish intent may be seen by others as something valiant or altruistic. Orson Scott Card points out that a "character is what he does, yes—but even more, a character is what he *means* to do."[16]

In *Behold the Dawn*, I made a list of the main characters and their various motives for their various actions:

Annan wants to die on the battlefield, because he feels the guilt for his crimes is too great a burden to go on carrying.

He wants to avoid an altercation with Bishop Roderic, because he knows Roderic's sins aren't his to punish.

He wants to put Mairead in a convent, so that he can go back to fighting in the tourneys.

Mairead wants to escape the horrors she's endured in the Holy Land.

She wants to reach the convent, so she can start a new life after her husband's death.

She wants to find Matthias of Claidmore because Gethin the Baptist told her Matthias would save her from Bishop Roderic and Hugh de Guerrant.

Roderic wants to have his enemies assassinated to save his own neck.

Gethin the Baptist wants to force Annan to find Matthias of Claidmore, so they can wreak vengeance on Roderic for what Roderic did to Gethin back in the Abby.

Marek wants to finish his term of indentureship to Annan, because Maid Dolly is waiting for him back in Scotland.

Hugh de Guerrant wants to find Mairead and force her to marry him, because he's obsessed with her.

He wants to find Annan and kill him, because Annan humiliated him in a tourney fight.

Creating a character who acts in exciting and larger-than-life ways is wonderful, but unless this character also has a reason for these actions, he will ultimately fail to capture readers' attention. Giving a character a motive (which inevitably extends to a goal, which hopefully inspires an immediate obstacle, which fortunately creates innate conflict) is vital.

Without an awareness of Raskolnikov's motive, reprehensible as it is, for killing the old woman in Fyodor Dostoyevsky's *Crime and Punishment*, readers would never have stuck around for 600 pages. If we didn't understand Jane Austen's titular Emma's good intentions for her blundering interference in her friends' lives, we would have abandoned her after a few chapters. Even characters whose actions are definably good, such as Luke Skywalker or Clark Kent, become boring unless we understand the motives behind their behavior.

It's not enough to create a character who does interesting things. He must also do them for interesting reasons. This principle allows authors all kinds of exciting space in which to play. We can match motive to action to present a straightforward character (such as Luke Skywalker), but we can also create infinite layers of complexity and intrigue by presenting a character whose actions and motives don't always seem to align (such as Bruce Wayne in Christopher Nolan's Batman movies).

Unlike fiction, in which we have the tendency to generously dole out black and white designations, motives and actions aren't always clear in real life. Becoming aware of, and taking advantage of, these complex dichotomies can raise our fiction to a new level by deepening our characters, creating subplots, and, perhaps most importantly of all, offering readers stories they can sink their teeth into and chew on for a while. What reader wouldn't admit that one of the chief joys of fiction is the ability to look into the hearts of the characters, where we can learn about them through their motives as well as their actions?

Your character's motive is what fuels his desire for something, and his desire is what gives him a goal to strive toward. For example, in *Gone With the Wind*, much of Scarlett O'Hara's actions in the second half of the movie are the result of her motive to "never be hungry again." Her desire is for safety and security, and her resultant goal is to gain wealth and status.

If we boil fiction down to the essentials, what we find at the core of a story is the main character's desire for something. What your character wants is what fuels him through page after page of conflict. We've all heard the saw that without conflict, there is no story. But without frustrating the character's ability to get whatever it is he wants, there can't be any conflict. Your character must want something and want it badly. Otherwise, he's not someone readers will find interesting enough to follow around for hundreds of pages. He should have one strong goal, usually inspired directly by the inciting event and often motivated further by strong beliefs or past experiences, that will carry him throughout the book, probably right up to the end (although sometimes it's necessary for characters to completely change their goals at some point in the story). This is the goal the author must frustrate at every turn throughout the book.

George Eliot's masterpiece *Middlemarch* is a hefty tome of 800 pages. Most modern readers stand agape at the mention of a book so large, especially one about quiet town life in 19th-century England. No explosions or high-speed car chases in this book, and the hero isn't out to save the prime minister from assassination or prevent another war with France. So how does Eliot keep her readers' attention for so long? Quite simply, her book is a superb example of delayed gratification. Eliot endows her characters with strong motives, desires, and goals—then absolutely refuses to give them what they want. Most of the characters' goals and desires are simple enough. Dorothea Casaubon and Will Ladislaw want to be together. The banker Bulstrode wants to keep others from learning about his criminal past. Dr. Lydgate wants to pay off his debts and live in harmony with his wife. Mary Garth wants her quasi-fiancé Fred Vincy to start acting like a responsible human being. Eliot tantalizes readers by allowing the characters to get close to their goals, only to be pushed back again and again. The result? Readers keep turning page after 800 pages to discover if, when, and how these characters will accomplish their goals and get what they want.

Fiction is a journey of many words, with the inevitable destination being the seemingly out-of-reach desire of one or more of the characters. Sometimes that desire is a thing (a valuable statuette in Dashiell Hammett's *The Maltese Falcon*), a person (Ashley Wilkes in Margaret Mitchell's *Gone With the Wind*), a state of mind (peace in Milena McGraw's *After Dunkirk*), a victory (the defeat of the Shuhr in Kathy Tyers's *Crown of Fire*), an escape (from the oppression of the Japanese in Pearl S. Buck's *Dragon Seed*), or a place (the Inkworld in Cornelia Funke's *Inkheart*). Your characters' goals will be unique to your premise, but what *isn't* unique is the necessity of the character's burning, undeniable urge to reach that goal.

What a character wants is bound inextricably to the arc he will follow over the course of the book. The changes that transform him from who he was at the beginning of the book to who he is at the end will be the direct result of how he goes about getting what he wants, or perhaps how the course of the story *changes* what he wants. Character arcs are linked to the catalyst of change. You can chart a character's arc through the progression of the story by comparing his personality, his behavior, his personal values, and his beliefs at the beginning and end of the book. How have they changed? (And they *must* change, not just on the surface, but also within the character's personal mores.)

Creating a solid, memorable character arc requires several important ingredients:

- **Start out with a clear idea of who the character is at the beginning of the story.** What does he care about? What does he believe? How does he behave in certain situations?

- **Open with the character beginning from a place of imperfection or incompleteness.** Usually (but not always) a main character's arc will show him growing into a better person.

• **Give the reader concrete examples throughout the book, but particularly early on, of the behavior and beliefs the character needs to change.** If he's a selfish jerk, maybe he goes out of his way to be cruel to a bum on the street. If he's a coward, maybe he cringes in a closet while someone else is beaten and robbed.

• **Give the character the tools he needs to improve himself.** This can come in the form of a mentor's advice or even just the character's actions creating a situation he recognizes as untenable. Growth needs to be slow and steady throughout the middle of the book.

• **Save the moment of revelation so it coincides with the emotional and physical climax.** This isn't always possible, but when you can bring the climaxes of the outer and inner journeys together, the result is explosive (see the section "Inner and Outer Battles" on page 85).

• **Prove the character's inner changes through his actions.** It's not enough to have him vow to be a better person; he has to prove it to the reader. Sometimes you can find a nice parallelism by reversing his earlier actions. If he was cruel to a bum on the street in the earlier scene, perhaps he could go out of his way to buy a meal for a bum at the end of the story.

CONFLICT

Who says conflict is a bad thing? Who says world peace is the most important goal of humanity? Who says arguing with your little brother when you're a kid means you'll grow up to be an ill-mannered ruffian?

Not a writer.

You can break every rule and still have a whopper of a story—so long as you remember to throw in a dash of conflict. Or, actually, a heaping tablespoon or two would be preferable. And yet many inexperienced authors forget all about conflict when planning their stories. One of the most common problems I encountered in editing unpublished authors' manuscripts is a complete lack of conflict. Authors allow their characters to wander aimlessly about their pages, hardly speaking to other characters and rarely encountering any obstacle except (usually) a dreary world view. No matter how marvelous your character, your plot, or your writing, no reader is going to be able to resist yawning in boredom over the lack of conflict.

The simple fact is: fiction has its very basis in conflict. If the main characters aren't clashing, if there are no wars, if the aliens are content to stay unobtrusively in their own galaxies—then we really don't have much of a story, do we? If Elizabeth and Mr. Darcy hit it off from the beginning, we never would have experienced all that wit and sizzle in *Pride and Prejudice*. If the North and South had resolved their differences over a handshake, Scarlett O'Hara would never have needed to escape a burning Atlanta. And if the Martians had minded their own business back on Mars, Orson Welles could never have made history by freaking out thousands of people with his *War of the Worlds* radio broadcast.

How does an author manufacture this most precious of story ingredients?

Happily enough, conflict is one of the easiest (and most fun) bits of story to craft. Once you have your character's motive, desire, and goal in place, all you have to do to rain down conflict on his head is to start throwing up obstacles between him and his goals. We authors are really pretty mean folk. Here we are, creating characters whom we're supposed to love almost as much as our family and friends, and yet, every day, on every page, we make these characters suffer by refusing to give them what they want and need. Truth be known, we kind of enjoy making them suffer.

How can we grin at ourselves around our toothbrushes every morning and feel no shame for this blatant sadism? Very simply, because if we did, our characters would have no reason to exist, and we'd be out of a job. Conflict fuels fiction, and frustration fuels conflict. Every time the character (and the reader) begins to think victory and happiness are around the bend, the author has to find some way to circumvent them. (As authors, we often identify ourselves with our main characters, when, really, we are always taking the part of the antagonist: helping him in his battle to defeat the hero.) This sort of frustration is obviously necessary in thrillers and action stories, in which the characters' lives must be under continual threat in order to maintain suspense. But even cozy romances and leisurely literary novels demand frustrated characters.

How can you keep the stakes as high as possible for your readers?

- **Watch for lags**. If you find your character happy or at peace, chances are good he's not too frustrated. Unless you're using a temporary lull in the storm to emphasize the disasters to come, avoid these quiet, happy scenes. Not only do they interrupt the dramatic flow, they also tend to be boring.

- **Write a list of the ten worst things that could happen to your character**. Jot down all your ideas, no matter how far out. If you haven't come up with anything feasible by the end of the list, write ten more. So long as the characters are always guessing, you can also keep the readers in the same state of suspense.

- **Vary the intensity**. Don't get so caught up in the need for frustration that you forget the importance of variety. Even the most thrilling race-'em, chase-'em, shoot-'em-up scenes will grow boring and lose focus if they aren't interspersed with low-key "sequel" scenes. Frustration doesn't always have to be a code-red alert; sometimes it can be only a niggling murmur.

- **Evaluate your scenes for frustration**. Take a glance at your outline and make note of what is frustrating the character in each scene. If you can't find a frustration—or if the source of frustration seems weak—grab your list of the ten worst things that could happen and start bolstering.

Whatever your chosen genre, frustration is the key to keeping characters and readers—and yourself—on their toes. If we're going to give readers what they want, we have to deny our characters what *they* want. As humans, we all know a little something about anarchy and chaos, and it really isn't much of a stretch to borrow some from real life and spread it around on the page—but just in case you're feeling stumped, here are a few suggestions.

Personality Clashes

This is the easiest (and, often, the best) way to throw a little conflict into the mix. Because character interaction is at the heart of any story, character clashes will produce your most consistent and interesting conflicts. The key thing to remember about clashing characters is they must clash for a realistic reason. Characters who get along perfectly for the first third of the story can't suddenly, for no apparent reason, explode into a manic fistfight. Instead, craft characters who naturally push each others' buttons. The most obvious form of relational conflict is that presented by the antagonist—the supremely evil being whose sole purpose in life is to wreak havoc in the universe and cause problems for your main character. But don't overlook the opportunities for conflict that exist on a much smaller scale in *all* of your minor characters—what fantasy author Janice Hardy calls "minitagonists."[17] Make sure your hero is surrounded by foils. If you find yourself with a minor character who affirms your protagonist at every turn, spice him up by throwing a little unexpected rebellion into the mix.

In her time-travel book *The House on the Strand*, Daphne du Maurier does a marvelous job of keeping the conflict rolling without ever resorting to a major bad guy. Most of the tension in the book is the result of, not a super-villain out to do unspeakable things to the hero, but instead the protagonist's wife. The hero's desire to keep his time travelling, via an experimental drug, a secret, and his wife's desire for him to leave England, take a high-paying job in America, drop his long-time friendship with the eccentric professor who invented the drug, and generally behave as a responsible husband and father put them at odds throughout much of the story.

An antagonist doesn't have to be someone who wants to kill the protagonist. An antagonist can be *anyone* who stands in the way of the hero accomplishing his goal, whether his goal is to save the world or just order a double latte. The more roadblocks you put between the hero and his goal, the more conflict—and the more tension—you're going to pour into your story.

Unexpected Situations

Many stories base their entire premise on the unexpected (think of the Pevensie siblings tumbling through the wardrobe into Narnia in C.S. Lewis's *The Lion, the Witch, and the Wardrobe* or young upper-class Jim Graham being sent to a Japanese prisoner camp in J.G. Ballard's *Empire of the Sun*). But, even if you don't go quite that far, you can still take advantage of the unexpected by forcing your character into situations and relationships that go against his inclinations or values. If you have a heroine who is terrified of speaking in public, why not put her in a situation where she has no choice? She'll either cave under the pressure or rise to the challenge. Either way, the reader will be hooked.

High Stakes

Readers aren't interested in stories about characters who sail through life, never encountering hardship, danger, or sadness. Rip your characters apart, put them under excruciating pressure, and then when things look like they couldn't possibly get any worse—make sure they do.

One of the easiest ways to raise the stakes is to create a tight timeline for your story. Even if your hero has a strong goal, readers are likely to lose interest if your character has all the time in the world to achieve that goal. Giving your characters a deadline—and suitably disagreeable consequences if they fail to meet it—ups the ante and keeps readers glued to your story. The classic World War II movie *The Guns of Navarone*, directed by J. Lee Thompson, presents a masterful use of the ticking clock. The heroes are on a suicide mission to destroy two huge guns in a German fortress. From the very beginning, they're on a tight schedule. If they don't blow up the guns in just a few days, hundreds of men stranded on the island of Kyros and everyone in the ships sent to rescue them will be killed. You'd think that would be tension enough, but scriptwriter Carl Foreman took things one step farther. Halfway into their mission, with a wounded man on their hands and half their supplies destroyed, the team members get word the deadline has been moved up a full day. Their already suicidal mission now looks completely impossible. Viewers are on the edge of their seats—and right in the palm of the filmmaker's hand.

Putting a time limit on your character's goals—whether that goal is to destroy an enemy base or just buy groceries—brings a whole new level of tension to your story. If your story takes place over a course of weeks, try shortening the timeline to days—and watch that ticking clock energize both your characters and your readers.

Inner and Outer Battles

Both inner and outer battles are necessary to produce well-rounded, memorable characters. When these battles are present in every scene, authors are able to use them to simultaneously advance the plot and develop their characters *within* the plot. In other words, conflict has to occur not just on the larger scale of the novel (whether that be a family crisis or World War III), but also on the smaller theater of the character's inner life. Every scene must include the outer battle (the physical reaction to conflict) and the inner battle (the psychological and emotional reaction to events). Any scene that lacks one or the other is teetering on the Cliff of Not Enough Conflict.

Combining the external conflict with the hero's internal conflict offers several benefits, including variation of the conflict within your story, heightened stakes, and, often, a more enduring resolution. The most powerful stories are usually those that bring the external and internal conflicts to a climax at the same time. The 2003 film adaptation of *Peter Pan* did a marvelous job of this. The physical conflict comes to an exciting, swashbuckling apex when Pan arrives to save Wendy and the Lost Boys and duel it out with Captain Hook for good and all. In itself, the external conflict offers the viewer all kinds of enjoyable tension and its subsequent payoff. But if the movie stopped at that—if it failed to bring Pan's internal conflict into play as well—it would ultimately have fallen flat.

Because the film used the frame of physical conflict to force Pan to face his inner demons, walk with them to the brink of destruction, and then rise up to conquer both them and, as a result, Captain Hook and the pirates as well, it was able to use both elements of conflict to strengthen each other and to present the viewer with a solid and resonant finale. The external conflict was able to give the internal conflict an exciting and dangerous setting, while the internal conflict was able to give the external conflict a deeper meaning. Working hand in hand, they present an unstoppable force of storytelling.

Balance

Although it's vital every scene contain some level of conflict, it's also important to monitor the general flow of that conflict. You have to open your story with enough conflict to grab the reader's attention, then continue building on it to keep him reading. But you don't want to pour on the danger and the distress so thick in the beginning that you run dry by the end of your story. Using fore-shadowing and tension, build your conflict at a steady rate of increase until you reach the high point of the climax.

Stories are about balance. A tale without conflict is going to be about as boring as watching condensation dissipate. But a tale that never pauses to let its characters (or its readers) catch their breath is boring in its own way. We have to find ways to adjust the level of the conflict. We have to give our characters a chance to slow down and get their thoughts gathered for the next attack. Stories must consist of both large- and small-scale battles. Mix things up. Throw in a variety of conflicts in all colors, shapes, and sizes, and keep both your characters and your readers guessing.

Forget what the peace pundits (not to mention your mother) say, and heap on the conflict. Peace and quiet never get an author anywhere.

THEME

Theme is a slippery concept. The prevailing thought among writers is that if you apply any deliberate force to your theme, you'll end up with a heavy-handed Aesop's fable. On the other hand, a story without a theme will be shallow escapism at best and an unrealistic flop at worst. Theme is very possibly the single most important facet of a memorable story. Vivid characters, witty dialogue, and killer plot twists can carry a story by themselves, but, without theme, they will never deliver the story's full potential.

Common wisdom insists fiction is meant to entertain, not preach. The novel isn't a soapbox for our religious, political, social, or philosophical views, and if we try to use it as such, we're likely to sacrifice our stories and alienate our readers. And yet, ironically enough, many of the world's most beloved pieces of literature are stories with blatant moral messages. We enjoy stories that challenge us and inspire us. We read to be entertained, but many of us also read to learn, to grow, and to stretch our horizons. This kind of depth is found only in stories that are profoundly honest, and stories can never be honest if their authors aren't willing to lay themselves open on the page and pour out their deepest convictions and most passionate beliefs about the human experience.

As an author, your most powerful gift is your unique and integral view of the world. When you strip fiction down to its essentials, the author's viewpoint is all there is. He may mask it artfully in the colorful garb of diverse characters and impartial dialogue, but if he's not willing to share with his readers his own passionate worldview, he's not giving them anything more than fluff.

So does this mean we should drag out soapboxes and start haranguing our readers into converting to our own viewpoints? Absolutely not. Nothing turns fiction readers off faster than a condescending author who preaches at them. Incorporating a message into our stories does not mean spelling out beliefs and arguments. Instead, it's a matter of choosing strong themes in which we fervently believe, creating multi-dimensional characters who struggle with the gray areas of life along with the rest of us, and crafting a plot that forces us to ask the hard questions. Someone once said being a novelist isn't about offering answers; it's about asking questions.

People are sometimes afraid of sharing too much of themselves in their writing. But let's be blunt: If you're worried about this, why write in the first place? What is fiction if not an intimate glimpse into someone else's heart and soul? Whether your stories are read by two people or two million, your writing is your legacy to the world. Make it worth sharing. Write yourself a list of the subjects, issues, and beliefs you'd fight and die for. If none of the items on your list make their way into your fiction, you should be asking yourself *why not?*

Use Characters to Share Theme

If you concentrate too much on theme, you risk alienating your audience through moralizing. But if you squelch all thoughts of theme, you're likely to rob your story of its central life force, its heartbeat, its *meaning*. So what's a writer to do?

As with almost every aspect of story, character is, once again, the key to making your theme come to unforgettable life. Theme is the lesson your characters will have learned (or failed to learn) by the end of the story. The best of themes well up effortlessly and even unconsciously from the heart of the characters' actions and reactions.

In Joseph Conrad's classic *Lord Jim*, the saga of a young sailor who is haunted by his one cowardly act, the theme could perhaps be summed up as "the repercussions of betrayal." Because the theme is a natural outflow of Jim's initial action (saving his own life instead of aiding his ship's drowning passengers) and his subsequent reactions (fleeing in shame, hiding out on an Indonesian island, and, ultimately, learning from his initial mistake and refusing to save his own life when the island comes under attack), Conrad's views on the subject can never be construed as moralizing or off-point. Indeed, the theme is at the very heart of the novel. Without it, *Lord Jim* would have been a rambling tale about the journeys of an ambiguous and forgettable young man.

The key to strong theme is strong character progression. The changes your character undergoes in the chapters between the inciting incident and the climax will define your theme. But these changes must flow naturally *from* the characters. If Conrad hadn't presented Jim as an idealistic young man who desperately regretted his actions aboard the *Patna*, the ending in which Jim chooses to sacrifice himself on the island would never have rung true. His transformation would have come across as forced and unrealistic, Conrad would have been guilty of moralizing—that blackest of authorial sins—and *Lord Jim* would never have reached its classic status.

How to Discover Your Theme

How do you go about implementing theme? Or perhaps the better question is: *Should* you go about implementing theme? Many writers avoid deliberate thoughts of theme while constructing their outlines and writing their first drafts. Many enter their stories with little or no intention for a specific theme, until, somewhere in the middle of the novel, the characters do or say something that dangles the scarlet thread of theme in front of the delighted author's nose.

Although I have never gone so far as to ignore theme (from the moment of a story's conception, I have my eyes stretched wide to catch that first glimpse of a possible theme), I do believe the single most important trick for capturing the sometimes elusive and always ephemeral theme is to pour yourself into creating authentic characters who react to their various crucibles in authentic ways.

Thanks to your outline, you know where the story will end before you ever write your first draft. Because you'll be able to see your plot progression and character arcs at a glance, you'll be able to identify your theme early on. Most stories offer a variety of themes, but you'll want to ask yourself the following questions in order to discover and strengthen the most prominent thematic thread:

- **What's the main character's internal conflict?** In most novels, this is a question that gets answered early in the outlining process, since it will drive the entirety of the story.

- **Which of the main character's views will change as a result of the story's events? How and why?** This is where you'll find the underlying force of your theme. Your character's views will define his actions, and his actions will define the story.

- **How will the main character demonstrate his respective views and attitudes at the beginning and the end of the story?** This is an extension of the previous question, but it is vital because, as we discussed earlier in regard to character arc, its answer will prove the changes to the reader.

- **Is there any particular symbolism that can reinforce the theme and the character's attitude toward it?** Like theme itself, symbolism is often overstated and generally better when culled organically from your unconscious mind. For example, sometimes you'll find yourself using a particular color or image to represent something. If the symbol proves effective, you can later go back and strengthen it. (Refer to the section "How to Strengthen Your Theme With Symbolism" on the following page.)

- **How can you use the subtext (the unstated) to exemplify the theme, so you won't have to spell it out for the reader?** When it comes to theme, the unstated is almost always more powerful than the direct. In real life, when we find ourselves learning lessons and changing views, we can't always immediately define the changes in precise language. And neither should your character. Lord Jim didn't have to *tell* us his actions on the island were a direct result of his earlier cowardice; the connection was obvious from the subtext and would, in fact, have weakened if Conrad mentioned it outright.

Once you've answered these questions, you should have some interesting ideas to include in your outline. My results for *Dreamlander* ended up looking like this:

Weakness: Chris Redston is selfish and irresponsible: He spends his life in search of the next big adrenaline trip, not really caring whom he lets down or hurts along the way.

Who is he hurting? His dad, Joe, random bystanders, Brooke, Lisa, Mike.

What does this character want? Chris wants to make the dreams stop.

What does this character need? To take responsibility for his actions and sacrifice himself for the good of others.

What does he know at the beginning? That people shirk

their responsibilities and hurt you, and that life is always just one step away from catastrophe, so you might as well live it to the hilt. Excitement kills the pain and proves you're still alive. If you never act responsible, then no one will expect you to be responsible, or be hurt when you fail to be responsible. (His fear of injuring others is buried deep in his unstated psyche. He would never *tell* you that.)

What is he *wrong* about in the beginning? He thinks the best way to avoid hurting people is to avoid responsibility. He thinks the only way to feel alive is to risk his life.

What will he learn at the end? To take responsibility for his actions and act for others above himself.

Hero's central problem: The realization that taking responsibility isn't just a flippant decision; sometimes it's a soul-deep commitment.

Thematic principle: Force an irresponsible young man to learn responsibility when his actions endanger two worlds.

Theme: If you're going to succeed as a human being, you have to take responsibility for your actions, even if it means losing what you love most.

How to Strengthen Your Theme With Symbolism

The use of symbolism in fiction is more difficult to learn than you might think, perhaps in large part because, when done well, symbols are almost invisible within the framework of the story. Those that aren't invisible often feel heavy-handed or even clichéd, such as the inevitable use of the American flag as a symbol of inspiration in war movies. Like the flag, some symbols are almost universal, and we utilize them to evoke reader emotions without even realizing what we're doing. For instance, springtime is often used to symbolize new growth, redemption, or resurrection.

The most powerful and unique symbols are those that flow effortlessly from your story. We find a good example in the 2000 movie *The Patriot*, directed by Roland Emmerich. After his son is murdered by a British colonel, plantation owner Benjamin Martin, played by Mel Gibson, salvages the boy's toy soldiers from his burning home, so he can melt the lead into musket balls. The toy soldiers appear throughout the movie, underlining the character's mixed emotions of loss, grief, anger, vengeance, and eventually a desire to fight for the cause his sons believed in.

This, by itself, is an effective use of symbolism. However, the film's *coup de grâce* is the moment, right before the climactic battle scene, when the main character melts down the final soldier into a final musket ball, which he will use to shoot the antagonist. It's a superb use of symbolism that is powerful without being obvious, subtle without being ambiguous, and flows naturally from the story's plot.

The power of thematic symbols lies in their ability to drive home a point via subtlety and repetition. This is exactly what Kurt Vonnegut does so well in his revered anti-war novel *Slaughterhouse-Five*. This strange novel is stripped down to stark essentials in a way that makes Vonnegut's repetition of thematic motifs particularly striking. He repeats certain phrases and images throughout the book, with an almost poetic variation, using both the blatant repetition and the subtle reinforcement of theme to drive his motifs deep into the reader's mind. In particular, he repeatedly uses the phrases "blue and ivory" to evoke cold, "mustard gas and roses" to describe foul smells, and, famously, "so it goes" to underline the tragedies referenced or described in the story.

Although some may argue that Vonnegut repeats his phrases to the point he compromises his subtlety, his book is nonetheless a conspicuous example of how a few evocative and memorable phrasings, carefully repeated for emphasis, can take a thematic experience into deeper waters, forcing readers to look beyond the obvious to the message behind the motifs.

Story without theme is like ice cream without milk. But to be effective, theme must be organic. Like all the finer points of writing, theme is an art worth mastering. If you can get a handle on your theme while in the early outlining stages, you'll be able to strengthen the entire arc of your story, and, by the time you're ready to write the first draft, the characters, plot, and theme will sing in perfect harmony.

Chapter Five Checklist

- ☑ Identify your characters' motives, desires, and goals.
- ☑ Decide how you can frustrate your character's desires and goals to create conflict.
- ☑ Make a list of the antagonistic forces that will counter your protagonist.
- ☑ Identify the themes already present in your story, select the most prominent one, and decide how you can strengthen it throughout the story.
- ☑ Keep your eyes open for possible symbols you can use to reinforce your theme.

ASKING THE AUTHORS

Bio: The author of the Joe Box mystery series (RiverOak) and the thriller *Heading Home* (Sheaf House), John Robinson spent three years teaching fiction tracks at Glorieta, a nationally ranked writers' conference. Visit him at johnrobinsonbooks.com.

Can you describe your outlining process?

Usually, my outlines are quite short—a couple pages in a yellow legal pad. It's more of a "primary plot point" type of docu-ment, giving me a story arc to follow. Secondary plot points, as well as ancillary characters, seem to show up on their own. Sometimes they bring peanuts.

What is the greatest benefit of outlining?

It helps me see the big picture and keeps me from getting bogged down in tar pits or rabbit trails that lead nowhere.

What is the biggest pitfall of outlining?

The biggest potential pitfall, I think, is to make an outline so rich and so detailed it sucks the life out of the story. I heard a very well-known writer speak at a conference several years ago, and he told the group his New York house required him to submit a forty-page outline for his next novel. *Forty pages.* Man, by that point you might as well go ahead and write the story!

Do you recommend "pantsing" for certain situations and outlining for others?

I tried pantsing. Once. The result was astoundingly bad. At the end of two hours of writing I had a bunch of stuff on a page, but no story could be found. Maybe it's just the way my brain works, but for me, an outline is not only a road map, it's a GPS. Without one, I'm soon driving down a one-way street at midnight in a bad part of a strange city. No thanks!

JOHN ROBINSON

What's the most important contributing factor to a successful outlining experience?

Just determining to sit down and hammer the silly thing out. Toiling over an outline ranks right down there with learning multiplication tables: drudgery, and then some. But once it's finished, then you can hand the story over to your creative side and let fly!

"Your character's backstory should feel to you that it doesn't 'end' where the story proper begins. It needs to still be there, under the surface. And if it's strong enough it will help immeasurably in creating a powerful [story]."

—*Pauline Kiernan*[18]

6

CHARACTER SKETCHES, PT. 1:
EXPLORING BACKSTORY

NOW THAT YOUR General Sketches have given you a good idea of your plot progression and story arc, and now that you've filled in the obvious plot holes, it's time to work on Character Sketches—beginning with backstory. When Ernest Hemingway spoke about the dignity of an iceberg being "due to only one-eighth of it being above water,"[19] he was speaking about the importance of the part of the story that isn't told. Those seven-eighths underwater are the ballast for the tiny bit that juts up to glisten in the sun. More often than not, those seven-eighths are composed of one of the most important facets of any tale: backstory.

Backstory, of course, is basically self-explanatory. It's the story that goes in *back* of the real story. It's the story before the story, the unseen history that informs all of your characters' decisions and actions. As such, it's understandably vital to the progression and consistency of your tale. Particularly during this modern trend of beginning stories *in medias res* (in the middle of things), a deep and full-bodied backstory is every whit as important as the story itself.

By this point in the outlining process, you should have a basic idea of the major plot points. You know who your heroes are, you know what they're after, and you know some of the things they must accomplish to reach their goals. But your concept of who they are and what, in their individual pasts, has shaped them into the people you need them to be, is probably foggy at best.

Before you can tell others your story, you have to tell *yourself* its prequel. I begin writing my characters' backstories with no other intention than figuring out where my story proper needs to go. The exhilarating part of all this is that the backstory usually takes on a life of its own and transforms my previously shallow concept of my stories into something much bigger. That little chunk of ice floating around in my imagination swells into a looming iceberg.

Within backstory, we find the motivations in our characters' lives:

- The inability to measure up to his younger brother, which fuels Peter Wiggin's anger and ambition (the Ender's Shadow series by Orson Scott Card).

- The long-harbored guilt for brutal war crimes, which impels Benjamin Martin to avoid joining the American Revolution (Roland Emmerich's movie *The Patriot*).

- The long years of loneliness, which influence John Barratt to accept the compulsory swapping of roles with his French lookalike (*The Scapegoat* by Daphne du Maurier).

In some lucky instances, the backstory takes over completely, as in Milena McGraw's *After Dunkirk* and Audrey Niffenegger's *The Time Traveler's Wife*.

The key to crafting stories with many layers—stories with depth and ballast—is to never ignore the blank spaces in your characters. Don't let them get away with telling you only what they must to make the story work. Search out the shadows in their pasts, discover their parents, their childhood friends, their catalysts. Don't just accept that your main character is a cop; find out *why* he became a cop. Don't just slap a scar on your heroine; discover *where* the scar came from.

USING YOUR INCITING EVENT AS A LAUNCH PAD

So where do you start your backstory? The obvious answer is "at the beginning": Where was your character born? Who were his parents? What events in his childhood shaped his outlook? But, as we'll discuss in the "Reverse Outlining" section in Chapter Nine, sometimes a less intuitive method proves more effective in bringing clarity and focus to discovering your character's backstory. Instead of starting at the beginning, try starting at the moment when the backstory officially ends and the story itself begins: the inciting event.

The inciting event is the moment your character's world is forever changed. It knocks over the first domino in the line of dominoes that form your plot. It sets off an irrevocable chain reaction that will eventually lead your character to the maelstrom of your climax. This event shapes your character's existence throughout your book. This is the event your backstory must logically lead up to. By beginning with the inciting event in your hunt for the buried treasure in your character's past, you'll have a better idea of the type of questions you should be asking. Questions such as:

- What events in the character's past caused the inciting event?

- What shaped the character in such a way to make him respond to the inciting event as he does?

- What unresolved issues from his past can further complicate the spiral of events that result from the inciting event?

Maximize Your Inciting Event

Before we begin answering these questions, let's take a look at how to create an inciting event that will fuel your plot and drive your characters forward.

What Is an Inciting Event?

Bestselling legal suspense author James Scott Bell describes the inciting event as a doorway: "The key question to ask yourself is this: Can my lead walk away from the plot right now and go on as he has before? If the answer is yes, you haven't gone through the first doorway yet."[20]

What *Isn't* an Inciting Event?

Your story may include several important plot developments before you get to the inciting event. For example, in Ridley Scott's 2000 film *Gladiator*, the inciting event—the death of Roman Emperor Marcus Aurelius—doesn't occur until after several important scenes, including Aurelius's offering his throne to the protagonist. Even though the preceding scenes are important, they do *not* irrevocably change the character's world.

Where Should the Inciting Event Occur?

Generally speaking, the inciting event should occur not quite a quarter of the way into your story. Setting it this late in the story allows you to appropriately pace the introduction of your character, his personal problems, and his normal world, so readers will sympathize with him and understand the stakes when the inciting event blasts into view. For example, *Gladiator*'s inciting event takes place after the character's normal world has been established (via the opening battle and the main character's interactions with the emperor and other important characters).

What Constitutes a Powerful Inciting Event?

Inciting events are as widely varied as their stories. Not all inciting events have to be earth-shattering tragedies, such as the death of a loved one. They can be as simple as the character moving to a new town (*North & South* by Elizabeth Gaskell), taking a new job (*Twelve O'Clock High* directed by Harry King), meeting someone (*The Last of the Mohicans* by James Fenimore Cooper), or even buying a pet (*Marley & Me* by John Grogan). What all inciting events have in common is that they accomplish the following:

- **Directly influence the story to follow.** Robbing a bank may change the character's life, but it's not an inciting event unless the story that follows couldn't have happened without the robbery. For example, in *Gladiator*, the emperor's death puts his cruel and inept son, who hates the protagonist, on the throne. As a result, the protagonist suddenly becomes an enemy of the state, forced to run, and, eventually, to fight in the gladiatorial battles, which are reinstated by the new emperor.

- **Create conflict.** Because change is difficult for and even resisted by most humans, it usually causes an atmosphere of conflict. The more change an inciting event creates, the deeper the conflict and the more intriguing the story. In *Gladiator*, the emperor's death causes a chain of reactions that cements the animosity between the protagonist and the antagonist, creating conflict that creates more conflict—dominos falling in a perfect row until the conflict involves not just their personal feud, but the empire as a whole.

• **Grab the reader's attention.** Your entire premise turns around the inciting event, so go for something special. This is one of your most important opportunities to grab your reader's attention. Don't settle for something mundane. Patricide by a weeping son, such as we find in *Gladiator*, not only rivets viewers to the screen in horror, it also raises all sorts of interesting questions about the characters.

• **Should be followed by action.** A character's decision to take action doesn't become irrevocable until he acts upon it. The protagonist in *Gladiator* reacts to the emperor's death by refusing to serve the murdering son—and then must take the consequences of his actions when the new emperor massacres his family.

How to Write Backstory

In exploring backstory, you'll begin an in-depth exploration of your characters. The backstory *of your novel* is necessarily the composited backstory *of all your characters*. Your characters' backstories represent the disparate paths that will lead them all to the intersection of your inciting event. You may use the methods listed in the next chapter to further refine your backstories, but, in the beginning, precision isn't as important as freeing your creativity to explore all the possibilities. Haul out your notebook and pen (or whatever tools you've chosen because they offer the most creative freedom) and start scribbling.

The General Statement

Begin with a general statement about the character. In my backstory for Marcus Annan, the protagonist of *Behold the Dawn*, I wrote:

Annan is the hero of our story. He is a hired assassin, a professional soldier, and in general a tough character. Tacit and solid, with the raw strength to more than match three full-grown men, he is a fearsome opponent on any level.

He is currently in the employ of King Richard, as a member of his personal guard. He came to that position by way of Richard's admiration of his fighting prowess at a fight in the lists during the trip East.

Unbeknownst to Richard, Annan has also been offered the job of assassinating either the King himself or the King's new Queen, Berengaria of Navarre. He was approached, before the King's vanguard ever embarked from England, by Bishop Roderic's emissary, and offered a hefty sum for killing the King.

At the time, this was everything I knew about the character and the inciting event. I used this information as a foundation to explore Annan's motivations and history. At this early stage in the story, I had only the vaguest sense of who this character was and what he would have to do to reach the climax. Not until I began exploring his backstory did I truly come to understand him as a character—and, indeed, to understand that almost all my preconceptions about him were incorrect. Almost nothing in those original three paragraphs made it into the final story. He remained "tacit and solid," but in the final version of the story, he actually declares he is "never an assassin." After further exploration of both Annan and the other characters' backstories, it turned out the bad guy Roderic of Devonshire, not Annan, was in King Richard I's retinue. And, in fact, King Richard's involvement in the story ended up being limited to a single scene.

This, in itself, is a fabulous example of why outlining is so valuable. An outline offers an indispensible amount of flexibility. Had I entered my first draft with these misconceptions about my character and my plot, I might have written half the book before realizing I was headed down the wrong road. The freedom found in crafting a backstory—and, indeed, *every* part of the outline—is the realization that nothing is set in stone. Explore every side alley, leave no stone unturned, and never be afraid of changing your story, no matter how radically, when a better idea comes along.

Exploration of Influencing Characters

After writing your general statement, you can progress to an exploration of the character's past. I generally begin with my character's place and date of birth, then move on to the relationships that have defined his life. Who are his parents? What are *their* backstories? Although, obviously, I don't have time to explore the parents' backstories in the same depth as the main character's, I want to get a sense of the people who influenced the protagonist's early life, particularly if his parents play an important role in the story proper. For example, in *Dreamlander*, the protagonist Chris Redston's relationship with his alcoholic father is key to his own character development. Because the father was an important character, I was willing to devote several paragraphs to him:

> His dad was a worker at the Motorola factories and moonlighted as a moderately successful writer of detective mysteries (his series was called *Jack Hansen, P.D.*). He was a bluff, handsome man, a good dad, and a loving husband—until the car accident that killed his wife and younger daughter. Chris broke his leg and cut open an arm that went through the window glass. Lisa, Chris's older sister, suffered a minor concussion. Paul walked away with only minor bruises.
>
> After that, Paul hit the bottle, barely hanging onto his job until Chris was in high school. Lisa took Chris in until he graduated. Neither of them maintained a good relationship with their dad. He was never mean—just self-absorbed in his guilt and his booze.

You'll also want to explore your character's relationship with his siblings and other important figures. In Marcus Annan's case, the prominent figure in his youth wasn't his father, but Lord William of Keaton, the knight to whom he was apprenticed. The depth to which you explore your character's early relationships will depend on how integral each relationship seems to the story. Explore anything that looks like it might offer a crucial event in your character's past or a grain of truth about his motivations.

Exploration of Education, Jobs, and Travel

How has this character spent his life? What's his level of education? What jobs has he held? Where has he traveled?

The answers—or lack of them—may be portals to important discoveries about your character's past. In researching Chris's backstory, I learned his job as a foreign correspondent for an international magazine had given him plenty of opportunities to travel—and to escape his father. In Annan's case, I stumbled across some shocking revelations: most notably that Annan had spent time, as a young man, in a monastery:

> After Annan's sister-in-law (and the twins she was pregnant with) were accidentally killed in a fight between Annan and his brother, a grief-ridden Annan joined a severe clan of monks to mend his ways and make up for his sin. His parents, even his brother, and especially Lord William of Keaton, were opposed to his ending such a promising career as a knight. But Annan cut off communications with them all.

That monastery—which I had no notion of prior to writing Annan's backstory—became the catalyst for the entire book. It changed everything I thought I knew about both the characters and the plot.

Exploration of Personal Epochs

Although every detail in a backstory is important, since it contributes to the author's understanding of his characters and plot, what you're *really* looking for as you explore your characters' histories are the epochs, the catalysts, and the notable events that have marked your characters' lives, for better or worse, in ways they'll never forget.

Usually, each backstory I write provides at least one nugget that transforms my understanding of the character: the car accident that tore Chris's family apart, the time Annan spent in the monastery and the secrets he carried away from it. These are the bits of gold you're searching for. The deeper you dig, the more likely you are to strike a rich vein, so don't let yourself get off easy with a few sentences: "Sam was born in Massachusetts. Married his high-school sweetheart after college. They have two kids. He works as an accountant." That kind of backstory gives you no insight into Sam's character and no treasure trove to fund a luxurious plot.

Often, my backstory ends up being just as complex and detailed as the story itself. A relatively small amount of this backstory will show up in the novel, but this kind of in-depth background information provides an incredibly strong foundation. And the bits of backstory that *do* make an appearance will add extra sparkle to your story.

USING BACKSTORY CORRECTLY

The best backstories are those that influence a story without obstructing it. Backstory is often misunderstood, mostly because it has gained something of a bad reputation through misuse. As writers, we should neither underestimate this crucial storytelling technique, nor allow it to overwhelm our main stories. There's a time and a place where backstory belongs—and a time and place where it doesn't. Sometimes the only person who needs to know the backstory is the author.

It's tempting to believe our readers are every bit as fascinated with our characters' backstories as we are. But don't be fooled. Readers are only interested in *what's gonna happen next*. If your character's favorite cat getting stuck in a tree when the character was six doesn't affect *what's gonna happen next*, readers couldn't care less. So how do you tell about the cat in the tree without boring your reader into closing the book?

We need look no farther than Alexandre Dumas's fanatically loved classic *The Three Musketeers* to find a masterful presentation of backstory. Athos, the de facto leader of the three musketeers, has a secret in his past. It's a grim, astonishing, fascinating secret, and, as such, we might expect Dumas to have revealed it to the reader right away. Instead, Dumas holds back the secret for almost half the book, so he can deliver Athos's backstory at the most poignant moment possible. And when he does reveal the secret, he gives the

108 — K.M. WEILAND

reader all he needs to know in a quick scene of dialogue that allows the story to proceed at full speed.

Dumas's mastery of backstory teaches us a couple lessons:

- Hint early on that your character *has* a backstory, but don't reveal what it is until the last possible moment, right before the information becomes crucial.

- Instead of indulging in lengthy flashback scenes that stall your momentum, present the backstory in a powerful punch with as few words as necessary.

Another masterpiece of effective backstory is Fred Zinneman's classic western *High Noon*, a movie that uses a rich and complex backstory to further the plot without overwhelming it. A viewing of *High Noon* teaches us that:

- **We must *give* our characters a backstory.** Every character in this movie has an intricate connection with the main character and the events that have brought the villain back to wreak vengeance.

- **Sometimes the most effective backstories are those that are hinted at rather than told outright.** We're never told exactly what happened between protagonist Will Kane and the half dozen other main characters. We learn just what we need to know when we need to know it. You'll find no lengthy flashback scenes in this story, and the result is a deepening of characterization that never slows the plot.

Backstory is there only because *something* had to come before Chapter One. It's never the point of the story and, when we dwell on it too much, we risk deviating from our plot and testing our readers' patience with our meandering and bloviating. Spending the necessary time to discover the depths of your story's underwater iceberg, and then realizing how to properly use it to keep the rest of your story floating (instead of pulling it under), will pay rich dividends when the time comes to outline your novel's plot.

Chapter Six Checklist

- ☑ Identify your inciting event.
- ☑ Write a general statement about your character.
- ☑ Explore the influencing characters in your protagonist's life.
- ☑ Explore your character's education, jobs, and travel.
- ☑ Explore your character's personal epochs.

ASKING THE AUTHORS

Bio: The award-winning and bestselling author of the historical romance novels *The Preacher's Bride* and *The Doctor's Lady* (Bethany House), Jody Hedlund received a bachelor's degree from Taylor University and a master's from the University of Wisconsin, both in Social Work. Visit her at jodyhedlund.blogspot.com.

Can you describe your outlining process?

First, I brainstorm for *plot ideas*. As I begin the research for a new book, I keep a running list of potential plot points. I jot down any and everything that looks interesting. I usually fill several notebook pages with all kinds of wild and crazy ideas.

Second, I brainstorm for my *main characters*. Again, as I read and research for the new story, I start writing down things I'd like to use for my characters. I keep a running list of possibilities in a notebook. Gradually, each character begins to take shape. Then, I transfer all the qualities I want to keep into my extensive character worksheets.

Third, I make a *rough outline* of my plot. From my brainstorm list, I pick and choose the "set pieces" or the most vital events in the story. I put those events in order and begin to fill in the other scenes that must happen to get from one major event to the next.

Fourth, I get to the point where I'm ready to write a *short paragraph for each chapter*. The paragraphs are not complex but are fleshed out enough that I can see in each a clear beginning, middle, and end to my story.

What is the greatest benefit of outlining?

The outline gives me a road map. I know the destination and a few of the major stops along the way (those "set pieces"). The rough map keeps me focused as I drive the story along.

JODY HEDLUND

What is the biggest pitfall of outlining?

The biggest pitfall is being too rigid. Just because we have our destination in mind doesn't mean we have to know every inch of ground we're going to cover to get there. As we move forward, we need to let our creativity have room to take our story onto new paths, perhaps more thrilling and winding and adventurous than we could have initially planned. In other words, if we stick too much to the original outline, we could stifle the creativity that comes as the story unfolds.

Do you recommend "pantsing" for certain situations and outlining for others?

I've never tried pantsing. I'm a tried and true plotter. Even when I write blog posts, I usually do best when I start with a simple outline.

What's the most important contributing factor to a successful outlining experience?

Keep your destination in mind for both the plot and character arcs. But be flexible. Be willing to take detours. Be on the lookout for the stops and scenery you may not have anticipated in the outlining phase. Enjoy the journey and let it show in your writing.

"Characters take on life sometimes by luck, but I suspect it is when you can write more entirely out of yourself, inside the skin, heart, mind, and soul of a person who is not yourself, that a character becomes in his own right another human being on the page."
—*Eudora Welty*

7

CHARACTER SKETCHES, PT. 2:
CHARACTER INTERVIEWS

IN THE WORDS of W. Somerset Maugham, "You can never know enough about your characters."[21] Do you know the color of your hero's eyes? Do you know where the bad guy went to college? Do you know your heroine's most embarrassing moment? Can you rattle off a list of your main character's idiosyncrasies? Typical expressions? Romantic history?

If any one of these questions has you fumbling for an answer, you're missing a prime opportunity to deepen your characters and expand your story. One of the most useful tools you can utilize is the "character interview." My own interview started out as twenty or so basic questions regarding physical appearance and personality issues. Now it contains over one hundred precise and penetrating questions, designed to get creativity flowing and characters talking.

The character interview is a vital part of my outlining process. I'll often fill up half a notebook with narrative answers to the most probing questions about my characters' relationships, beliefs, and secrets. I refer to these lists continually throughout the actual writing process, not only for on-the-spot inspiration, but for fact checking (How old was he when his mother died? Did he break his left or his right leg in that car accident?).

Below, you'll find the list of questions I use. (A printable version is available online in my free e-book *Crafting Unforgettable Characters: A Hands-On Introduction to Bringing Your Characters to Life*, available on my website at kmweiland.com/free-ebook.php.) Character interviews are a lengthy process, so you may only want to focus on the point-of-view characters, the antagonist, and maybe one or two important minor characters. This part of the outlining process should get your brain juices foaming and raise all kinds of interesting tangents and opportunities for deepening the plot.

CHARACTER INTERVIEW

Name:
> Does he like his name? What does his name mean to him?

Background:
> Birthday:
> Place of birth:
> Parents:
>> What was important to the people who raised him?

> Siblings:
> Economic/social status growing up:
> Ethnic background:
> Places lived:
>> Current address and phone number:

> Education:
>> Favorite subject in school:
>> Special training:

> Jobs:
>> Salary:

> Travel:
> Friends:
>> Lives with:
>> Fights with:
>> Spends time with:
>> Wishes to spend time with:
>> Who depends on him and why?
>> People he most admires:
>> How do other people view him?

Enemies:
Dating, marriage:
Children:
Overall outlook on life:
Relationship with God:
Does he like himself?
What, if anything, would he like to change about his life?
What personal demons haunt him?
Is he lying to himself about something?
Optimistic/Pessimistic:
Real/Feigned:
Morality level:
Confidence level:
Typical day:
Physical appearance:
Physical build:
Posture:
Head shape:
Eyes:
Nose:
Mouth:
Hair:
Skin:
Tattoos/piercings/scars:
Voice:
Clothing:
What people notice first:
How would he describe himself?
Health/disabilities/handicaps:
Characteristics:
Personality type:
Strongest/weakest character traits:
How can the flip side of his strong point be a weakness?
How much self-control and self-discipline does he have?
What makes him angry?
What makes him cry?
Fears:
What people, places, situations does he avoid?

Talents:
What people like best about him:
Interests and favorites:
    Political views:
    Collections:
    Favorite food/drink:
    Favorite music:
    Favorite books:
    Favorite movies:
    Favorite sports/recreation:
        Did he play in school?
    Favorite color:
    Childhood daydreams/current daydreams:
    Best way to spend a weekend:
    A great gift for this person:
    Pets:
    Vehicles:
Typical expressions:
    When happy:
    When angry:
    When frustrated:
    When sad:
    When afraid:
  Most used facial expressions and gestures (smirk, frown, wince, hand motion, shrug, eye contact):
Idiosyncrasies:
Laughs or jeers at:
Ways to annoy this person:
Ways to cheer up this person:
Hopes and dreams:
    How does he see himself accomplishing these dreams?
Worst thing he's ever done to someone:
Greatest success:
Biggest trauma:
Biggest embarrassment:
Cares about most:

Secrets:
If he could do one thing and succeed at it, what would it be?
He is the kind of person who:
What do you love most about him?
Why will the reader sympathize with him right away?
How is he ordinary or extraordinary?
How is his situation ordinary or extraordinary?
Core need:
Anecdote (defining moment):
History:

Although you can answer the questions by simply filling in the blanks (e.g., Overall outlook on life: Cynical), you can allow your imagination more freedom by working the problem out longhand in your notebook, writing down and fleshing out your every idea. For example, here's what I wrote about *Behold the Dawn*'s Marcus Annan, in response to "Strongest/weakest character traits" and "How do other people view him?":

> Annan's strong trait is the light of a moral core that refuses to be dampened despite the ashes of sin and despair heaped upon it. There is a line Annan will not cross. He has walked upon it many times, but he will not be pushed over.
>
> He has many weaknesses. His temper, backed by all of his formidable strength and power, is a weapon to be feared. He kills without thought, though, ironically, he is also quick to defend others. He is a man of conundrums. He kills and yet, for some things, he's willing to be killed. He hates, and yet he hates his hatred. He is a man of passion, yet also of discipline.
>
> Annan is not interested in being liked. He is interested in being effective. Nonetheless, on some occasions, he has been noted to make favorable impressions, either through his fighting skills or some flash of virtue, most frequently generosity. He's a good man to have at your side in a fight.

FREEHAND INTERVIEW

If your character turns out to be the closemouthed type who refuses to let you into his deeper psyche, try a "freehand interview." Instead of forcing your character into the rigidity of the set questions in a regular interview, just throw him onto the page and start asking him questions: *What's the matter with you? What are you hiding from me?* It's always surprising how many unexpected confessions you can drag out of your characters. Your freehand interview might end up looking something like this:

Author: Why are you being so uncooperative?

Character: Why are you asking stupid questions?

Author: Because I need you to do what I tell you. I need you to show some fight to your wicked stepmother, instead of just pouting and taking it.

Character: That is *so* easy for you to say. You don't know my stepmother. And besides I'm not just taking it. Somebody has to do the chores around here and take care of my baby stepsisters. If I don't do it, we'll all die in filthy misery.

Author: But why should *you* have to do everything? You've got your rights. Don't you think your stepsisters—not to mention your stepmother—should take their share of the responsibilities? Why shouldn't they have to sweep the cinders out of the fireplace every now and then?

Character: They're delicate.

Author: They're not delicate. They're pampered. If you got out of the way and stopped babying them and letting them walk all over you, maybe they'd actually grow up into responsible human beings.

Character: They need me. Without me, they'd never survive.

Author: They don't need you. They're *using* you.

Character: That is not true!

Author: Why do you need to be needed so badly?

Character: Because—I don't know—

Author: C'mon, say it.

Character: Because if they don't need me, they won't love me!

And, *voila*, suddenly you know something new and interesting about your character and her motivations.

ENNEAGRAM

In general, I'm not a fan of using personality tests (such as the popular Myers-Briggs Type Indicator) to flesh out characters. Trying to force a character to fit a personality framework, rather than allowing him to evolve organically, can leave you with a cardboard cutout, instead of a unique and compelling character. However, because of its simplicity, I occasionally utilize the enneagram to make sure my characters' personality traits (particularly strengths and weaknesses) are balanced. The enneagram is a typology of human personalities that aligns character traits to one of nine categories.

Enneagram Chart

Type	Ideal	Fear	Desire	Vice
1: Reformer	Perfection	Corruption	Integrity	Anger
2: Helper	Freedom	Unworthiness	Love	Vainglory
3: Achiever	Hope	Worthlessness	Being valued	Deceit
4: Individual	Origin	Commonness	Authenticity	Envy
5: Investigator	Omniscience	Uselessness	Competency	Avarice
6: Loyalist	Faith	Isolation	Safety	Fear
7: Enthusiast	Work	Boredom	Experiences	Gluttony
8: Challenger	Truth	Loss of control	Autonomy	Lust
9: Peacemaker	Love	Loss	Stability	Indifference

Visit booklaurie.com/workshops_flaw.php for an explanation of the enneagram designed specifically for writers. Not only is it fascinating reading, it can help you round out a character, summarize his personality, and identify his "fatal flaw." For example, in the early stages of discovering *Dreamlander*'s characters, I scanned the enneagram list and realized my protagonist Chris Redston was an Enthusiast, constantly in search of fulfillment and gratification through the next big adrenaline trip. Another main character, Allara Katadin, was a Reformer, burning herself up with guilt and anger over her failed attempts to make her world a better place. The enneagram didn't tell me new things about my characters, so much as it helped me put into concrete terms things I already knew.

Chapter Seven Checklist

☑ Interview your character.

☑ Write a freehand interview of your character.

☑ Use the enneagram to identify your character's personality and "fatal flaw."

ASKING THE AUTHORS

Bio: The author of the historical novels *Chase the Wind* and *Rightfully Mine* (Thomas Nelson), Aggie Villanueva is the founder of Promotion á la Carte, an author promotional service, voted #2 in Preditors & Editors' Promotion category. Visit her at promotionalacarte.com.

Can you describe your outlining process?

With ancient-history fiction I create a very short paragraph-style outline of what I already know of the story, and, as research advances, I make delightful discoveries and flesh out a detailed outline, written in text format, not numerical. Of course the outline changes and grows and becomes wonderfully complex during the year or so of research I usually need to be ready to write.

What is the greatest benefit of outlining?

Probably my own greatest benefit is the character definition that results from my triple-play outlining style: Outline/Research/Characterize. These are inseparable. First, I start researching every level of my historical period. This adds vitalizing details to the outline, which expands/changes because of the research. I simultaneously write volumes of first-person narratives by each main character, not about the story necessarily, but about a childhood memory they can't forget, a bio of themselves as if they're preparing it for a dating site, favorite things and why, etc. The characterization is simultaneous because it grows naturally out of the outlining and research. For instance, I might discover a little-known everyday life detail so pertinent to a scene in my outline that it totally changes it, all for the better, making my readers feel like they've always lived in that time period and known that character. Hand-in-hand outlining and research molds my characterizations.

And, of course, an outline comes in handy when a synopsis is requested. At that point, I create the numerical outline form from the reams I've written about the story.

AGGIE VILLANUEVA

What is the biggest pitfall of outlining?

A common pitfall for me comes from using the Roman numeral outline format. This system is so dry it can create a distance between me and my characters and my story that I'm unaware of. Beware of anything that can drive such a wedge.

Do you recommend "pantsing" for certain situations and outlining for others?

Though my outlines are so informal as to not even be recognizable as outlines, they are actually very detailed and exact. I've never really tried pantsing, since my fiction is historical and demands minute detail recall, which I could never accomplish with just my lil' ol' brain. But the triple-play style is almost more like writing a separate book, especially the first-person reams written "by" the main characters, and even some minor ones.

What's the most important contributing factor to a successful outlining experience?

Staying loose. Outline in the way most natural to you and your characters and your story, and even allow it to change from book to book if needed.

"You are always looking for ways to deliver character to your reader. One of the most important and ready ways of doing that is through the character's interaction with his or her city…. Because he is really contemplating himself."
—Michael Connelly[22]

8
DISCOVERING YOUR SETTING

SETTING IS SOMETIMES the neglected stepchild of the writing world. We lavish attention on our characters and plot, but don't always remember how powerful a fabulous setting can be. Some genres, particularly those that fall within the realm of speculative fiction, tend to give more attention to setting, simply because their stories require intensive world building. But whatever your genre, you can borrow a page from fantasy writers and watch and learn from their detailed and engaging settings. You'll be hard-pressed to find a better example than *The Final Empire*, the first book in Brandon Sanderson's Mistborn series. The unique world he creates in this story is exquisite in its detail and verisimilitude. But the true power of his setting is grounded in a couple of hard facts.

- **Fact #1:** This world plays a much bigger role than that of a mere backdrop, a two-dimensional painting on the stage behind the actors. If your settings aren't intrinsic to your stories to the extent of almost being a character unto themselves, you're wasting an important opportunity.

- **Fact #2:** Sanderson brings his setting to life through a deft administration of details: not too many, not too few. He highlights the details that are important—the unique and pertinent points—by exemplifying them through his characters' inter-actions with the world. The lesson we all need to learn from this is how to find just the right telling detail to similarly bring our own scenes to life for our readers.

Depending on the type of story you write, the setting may be little more than an afterthought, an arbitrary decision made simply because your characters have to live *somewhere*. In the best stories, however, setting is an inherent element in bringing to life not just the scenery but also the characters themselves. As such, it isn't something we can afford to overlook. Asking yourself the following questions during the outlining stage will strengthen the weak points in your setting construction and help you use it to its full potential.

IS YOUR SETTING INHERENT TO YOUR STORY?

In some stories, the setting is so important that to change it would mean changing the entire plot. In *Empire of the Sun*, J.G. Ballard's novelization of his boyhood in a Japanese POW camp during World War II, the setting, first in Shanghai, then in the civilian prisoner camp, cannot possibly be separated from the story itself. The power of the unique setting and the vivid word pictures in which Ballard paints make this book breathe. In contrast, the sequel *The Kindness of Women*, which takes place when the author/hero is a grown man living in England, fails to share the original's strong sense of place—and as a result never comes close to achieving the same power.

HOW DOES YOUR CHARACTER VIEW HIS SETTING?

Bestselling mystery author Elizabeth George points out that "through a character's environment, you show who he is."[23] The way your character interacts with the landscape around him, with the familiarities of his home, and with the broader scope of his city give you insight into the character himself. Does he hate where he lives? If so, why is he still living there? Did he grow up there? If so, how did it shape him? In his narrative reaction to these places, he's not just musing about the setting, he's revealing truths about himself.

DOES YOUR SETTING AFFECT THE MOOD?

Setting, more than any other facet of the story, allows us the most flexibility for creating mood and pacing. The ominous thunderheads gathering above the protagonist's cornfield, the forbidding chill around the abandoned shack on the side of the road, the stuffy air inside a funeral home—all these bits of setting serve to inform the reader of the mood you're trying to set.

ARE YOU USING TOO MANY SETTINGS?

Settings are more than scenery. They're the cohesive grounding— the foundation of the whole story—and as such they need to be used with sparing care. The most powerful stories are those distilled to their inherent ingredients by removing extraneous information that detracts from their potent focus. Introducing a slew of settings is much like introducing a slew of characters: The reader's attention fragments, and both the writer and the reader have to spend more time and effort to keep track of details and orient their emotional connection. Following are some tips for distilling your settings to the perfect number:

- **Choose your primary settings wisely.** Setting should never be an arbitrary decision. Instead of throwing your characters into the first locale that pops to mind, consider the needs of your story. You're going to be spending a lot of time in this setting, so you need to choose a place that will enhance the requirements of your plot.

- **Utilize and explore your primary setting.** Once you've decided upon an interesting setting, take advantage of it. If your character is in a prisoner of war camp, a spaceship, a cattle ranch, or a Victorian mansion, then use every nook and cranny to further your story and hold your reader's attention. Readers would much rather explore one fascinating setting than catch only a glimpse of half a dozen.

- **Combine settings.** Streamline your sub-settings by combining them wherever possible. Instead of sending your protagonist to a restaurant, a pub, and a food fair, try combining them. This eliminates the need to describe a new setting in every scene, allows your readers the satisfaction of returning to a familiar place, and presents deepening layers of possibilities with recurring minor characters.

- **Foreshadow settings.** Maintaining only necessary settings allows you rich opportunities for foreshadowing. When important scenes occur in familiar settings, it's that much easier to lay the groundwork in earlier scenes, thus bringing your characters full circle and providing a gratifying sense of closure for readers.

As one of the most important resources in your possession, settings need to be utilized wisely and frugally so they can bring their full impact to the story. Choose your settings carefully. Don't settle for the obvious answers. Look beyond clichés, and examine the needs of your story to find the most appropriate setting. Then juice it for every drop of usefulness. If you can bring the setting to life as a character in its own right, you'll be that much closer to creating a story your readers will never forget.

WORLD BUILDING

In many genres, the setting is little more than a necessary backdrop, culled from the author's real life or research for any number of necessary or arbitrary reasons. Before writing *Dreamlander*, my experience with historical fiction allowed me to drop all my characters into real-life settings. I didn't have to create settings; all I had to do was reconstruct them from my own memory (the Wyoming setting in *A Man Called Outlaw*) or my research (the European and Middle Eastern settings in *Behold the Dawn*). But when I embarked into the magical world of fantasy with *Dreamlander*, I was presented with a wonderful new opportunity: I was no longer constrained by the facts. Instead, I had the freedom to create an entirely new world where anything could happen.

In the face of all these possibilities, authors can easily become overwhelmed. Where do we start? How do we create a world that not only incorporates beautiful and fascinatingly bizarre elements, but also one that is solid and realistic in every detail, from landscape to government? The first, and hopefully most obvious, answer is to let your imagination run riot. Force yourself to think outside the box, to reject clichés, and to hunt down ideas that excite you with their color and originality.

But you're also going to want to get as specific as you can. The interview process you used in getting to know your characters can also be applied to your setting. Fantasy author Patricia C. Wrede has compiled a fabulously complete list of Fantasy Worldbuilding Questions, which you can find at sfwa.org/2009/08/fantasy world building-questions. I won't attempt to retread her ground, but below is an overview of subjects and questions to keep in mind as you develop your speculative setting:

What does the landscape look like?
  What kinds of plants grow here?
  What's the climate?
  What kinds of animals are present in this world?

What kinds of societies are found in this world?
  What kinds of clothing are in style?
  What moral and religious values define people's world views?
  What language(s) do they speak?
  What form of government is currently in place?

How advanced is technology?
  What forms of long-distance communication are used?
  What modes of transportation are available?
  How has technology affected entertainment and the arts?
  How has technology affected weaponry and modes of warfare?
  How advanced are the fields of medicine and science?

What are the natural laws of this world?
  Which natural laws are different from our world (e.g., gravity)?
  Is there a magical force in your world? How does it work? What are its limitations?

What kinds of people populate this world?
Are there different races?
How do customs differ between people of different races and citizens of different districts?
Do the ethnic factions get along?

What's the history of this world?
How many years of recorded history are available?
What historical epochs have shaped society?

Answer these questions just as you did those in the Character Interview. Let your imagination run wild as you record every idea— no matter how silly it may initially seem. What you come up with may look a bit like my answer regarding art and entertainment in *Dreamlander*:

Theater is in two different states: the elevated, refined, morally acceptable theater which is considered high art. This includes operas. The other is the bawdy barroom theater, which is frowned upon by good society. Dancing falls into the same categories: refined and accepted; bawdy and rejected. An artist's status depends entirely upon which group he falls into. Refined artists are revered; bawdy artists are looked upon as fallen members of society, but there is a growing part of the population that idolizes and adores them.

The refined arts are supported by the church and, more especially, by the king and his court. The bawdy arts are supported entirely by their clientele, mostly bar owners and the like. The refined arts have several lovely theaters in all the main cities, a few are commercial businesses, most are publicly owned. Bawdy arts are confined to bars and the like, with the performers traveling from place to place. Circuses are one of the few "lower" class entertainments not frowned upon by the church, and traveling troupes erect their tents from town to town.

Hawking is popular among the well-to-do, with the lower classes emulating with less expensive birds and dogs. Hunting is popular among all classes. Tourneys, jousts, and fights are popular among the Cherazii. Sports include wrestling, swimming, rowing, and rustif, a game much like hockey without the skates. Board games involving stratagem, such as chess, are popular. Youngsters play at jacks, bowling, and the like.

Even if you already have a good idea of the specifics of your world, taking the time to solidify your ideas by answering these questions can inject more life and realism into your setting and allow you to spot flaws and inconsistencies. And, even better, it's fun!

Chapter Eight Checklist

- ☑ Choose your setting(s).
- ☑ Write a quick list of ways you can use the chosen setting to deepen characterization.
- ☑ Combine and eliminate unnecessary settings.
- ☑ Answer the list of world-building questions.

ASKING THE AUTHORS

Bio: The author of the YA novels *Angel in the Shadows* (Eloquent) and *Angel in the Storm*, Lisa Grace does volunteer work with teens through her church. Visit her at lisagracebooks.com.

Can you describe your outlining process?

I start my outlines by listing a major plot and two subplots. My main character has to learn something by the end of the story. My subplots must thwart the main character from achieving her goal. From the subplots, I come up with an idea of who my secondary characters are, the ones who will help move along the plot and the action of my main characters. I also like (while I am in the writing process) to create some charts. One for switching from character to character and another for scenes. I write approximately a thousand words per scene, so for a 70,000 word book, I need seventy scenes.

What is the greatest benefit of outlining?

Outlining, which is a form of planning, gives me the chance to build tension, add symbolism, and balance the interaction between the characters and the plotlines.

What is the biggest pitfall of outlining?

Sticking too rigidly to your outline. One of my favorite characters in *Angel in the Shadows* popped up while I was writing a scene. Her addition helps move the action along and gives a new perspective of how to look at the world. If I'd stuck rigidly to my outline, my readers and I would be missing out.

Do you recommend "pantsing" for certain situations and outlining for others?

My writing style is short and sweet. Lots of dialogue, action, and just enough description to set the scene. I need a clear idea of where my scenes are going and what they are adding to the story. My "pantsing" occurs within the framework of

LISA GRACE

the scenes. I might add a scene I hadn't planned on because it is what the characters would naturally do next.

With my current work-in-progress, a historical, I have to outline to make sure timelines, locations, events, weather, battles, and real-life people all match up correctly with my characters. I couldn't write an accurate portrayal of the times in my fictional story without an outline.

What's the most important contributing factor to a successful outlining experience?

Laura Lippman, author of many award-winning novels and one of my mentors, is visual. She outlines by color coding (with Post-its® or index cards), on her wall. One for characters and POV, then another with scenes. She then looks at the pattern each creates. If the pattern isn't pleasing, she changes it.

I use lines and connect my scenes/characters as I go. If I have too many lines going in the same direction at the same time, I can see where I need to bring in the other characters/plots/scenes. To be successful in outlining, you have to do what works for you.

"Writing is a way of organizing experience, or of organizing something imagined, of making something perfect and beautiful—even something as small as one sentence—in a world that can be at times chaotic, wretched, ugly, and upsetting."
—*Patricia Highsmith*[24]

9

THE EXTENDED OUTLINE: CREATING A STORY

THE EXTENDED OUTLINE is where the plotting begins in earnest. Step by step, you're going to map out, in as much detail as possible (though without dialogue or narrative), every road stop in your story. In places, this plotting will go quickly; in others, you'll have to stop to work your way through iffy plot points and implausible character motivations. This step, by itself, can take several months, but because of the active, full-throttle creativity demanded, it's one of the most exciting and rewarding portions of storytelling.

I write my Extended Outline in my notebook, dating each entry and numbering each scene. Below are the first two scenes from *Behold the Dawn*'s outline, to give you an idea how it should flow. As you'll see, I ramble, digress, switch tenses, reject ideas, and generally let myself wander all over my imagination, having fun and seeking plot solutions that are both plausible and unexpected. I plan foreshadowing and sort out the whereabouts and mindsets of my various characters, keeping motives and goals at the forefront. My objective in constructing each scene is to nail down the prominent events, while still leaving lots of room for creativity and improvisation later on, when I actually write the scene. Very occasionally, if an appropriate line of dialogue strikes me, I'll include it, but, otherwise, I save the detail work, such as dialogue, description, and internal narrative, for the first draft.

1. I think I actually want the story to start a little before the story, so to speak. But I'm not sure how much before—with Annan accepting Roderic's assignment? With him in battle at Acre (no—because that's just action, there's no character identification and that's the most important part; I guess I could make it work, but it would take some effort to make it strong. It could be strong though)? Maybe as he's wounded? Maybe somewhere in between one of those?

I rather lean toward the first option, but I don't want to go too far back, and I definitely want a smooth transition to the battle, and then, when he's wounded, I see it as being kind of ethereal and unreal, cloaked in the fury of the battle. You know, sort of just drifting along through the dreamy memories of this battle, and then *boom* he wakes to a world of pain and Mairead's worried face.

2. So he wakes up in some sort of confinement, whatever the Saracens were using. (I have to find out if they took prisoners—I don't think they took many—and what they did with them when they didn't kill them.) He is wounded: probably a head wound, maybe a flesh wound in his shoulder or side. Nothing that will take too long to heal, but enough to keep him down for a bit, so Mairead can nurse him.

When he recovers a bit, he is taken to another cell to see Lord William of Keaton. Annan must have initiated the meeting, probably because he had an opportunity for escape, and he wanted to share it with Mairead because of her aid to him.

He doesn't know she's married, much less that her husband is his old mentor, William of Keaton, who is grievously wounded.

During Annan and William's reunion, I'll have to begin dropping hints about Annan's past. Not too much though—just a little bit.

William, knowing he's going to die and afraid of what Lord Hugh will force upon Mairead, once she is no longer attached, requested that Annan marry her, if only in name, and then help her escape to a convent in France that would be paid for with Lord William's legacy. Annan, although just a wee bit taken aback, agreed, out of his friendship with William, his sympathy for the lady, and the debt he felt he owed them.

So he sets about orchestrating an escape. I'm not sure if I want to utilize outside help in this or not. I don't like bringing in a character just for the sake of getting Annan loose, but without another person, I think we lose some of the urgency somewhere. I could introduce someone—or the instrument of someone—who will play a vital part later on. Marek doesn't know Annan's even still alive, so he's out. And I don't know that I want Gethin to be that wise to Annan's existence.

But then again... having an unknown rescuer puts a nice little question mark in there. And Gethin wouldn't necessarily have to know it's Annan he's rescuing. He could a) be just trying to release as many prisoners as he can (problem with that, though, is that we only want Annan and Mairead to get away), b) wanting to free the assassin because he needed him for some reason to get at Roderic (need a more concrete reason though), or c) he wants to get Lady Mairead and/or William out—Annan doesn't enter into it. It just ends up happening that "Lady Mairead and her husband" weren't quite who Gethin thought. That's good, esp. since Gethin will think, until he encounters them, that Annan is William. Double surprise for him, since, not only is it not William, but it's his old buddy Annan. And because Gethin wouldn't know of Annan and Mairead's marriage, and because he does know Annan's personality, he may be very condemning and antagonistic at first, doubly so if he doesn't know William is dead.

Okay, so thanks to Gethin, they escape (Annan would have tried to escape anyway, so it's still fine for him to offer that to William and Mairead).

Before we discuss plotting techniques any further, let's take a moment to go over a few preliminary steps and questions.

WHAT KIND OF STORY ARE YOU WRITING?

Now's the time to begin making concrete decisions about the form this story will take. What audience are you writing it for? What feel and tone do you want to present in the prose? Will it be fast-paced or leisurely? Will you write in past or present tense?

There's no such thing as the perfect novel. Perfection in art is unequivocally subjective. What one reader hails as perfection, another will throw across the room in disgust. As readers, our preferred reading experiences span the gamut from cuddly, reaffirming romances to gritty, life-challenging noir. And that's awesome. A world without variety would leave authors with very little of interest to write about.

Because the perfect novel will never exist, authors have lots of room in which to play around and find their niches. Therefore, the question isn't so much "how to write the perfect novel" as it is "how to write *your* perfect novel." A line of encouragement from literary agent Scott Edelstein has informed my writing for years now. He said, "If you're ever at a loss as to what to write about, ask yourself to imagine the one story, essay, poem, or book that you'd most like to read. Then write it."[25]

So what is *your* perfect novel? Examine your favorite novels and movies for elements that particularly grabbed you. Battle scenes? Romance? Humorous dialogue? Plot twists? Sad endings? Happy endings? Chances are the story elements that are important to you are already showing up in your work. If you can single them out, you can strengthen them and make them more intrinsic to your stories.

Who Is Your Audience?

It's essential to know your audience and to know what they expect from you. When, how, and if you decide to fulfill those expectations need to be educated decisions.

• How old is your audience?

- What gender is your audience?

- What ethnicity is your audience?

- What religious beliefs does your audience ascribe to?

Knowing the answers to these questions will help you decide how best to craft your story. If, upon reflection, your story doesn't seem to fit your audience, you either need a new story or a new audience. Sometimes it helps to select one person—someone who understands you and your worldview, but perhaps doesn't agree with you entirely. What would this friend think of your story? What would he like about it? Dislike? What would he tell you to change to make the story better? Hold this one reader in mind as you design your outline, and you'll be able to stay in touch with your intended audience, as a whole, as you craft your story. Writing to an audience is one of the inevitable joys and frustrations of the writing life. We can't avoid it, despite its pitfalls, but we can channel it by narrowing that audience to specificity.

What Point of View Will You Write From?

Narrative point of view (or POV) is something writers often take for granted. We come up with a story idea, sit down to write, and spend maybe all of thirty seconds debating between a first- and third-person POV. But this snap, arbitrary decision will influence every one of the 100,000-plus words to follow. It will be a deciding factor in the story's tone and narrative arc. It will control which scenes will be written and which will remain "off-camera." It will close certain doors and open others. In short, POV is often the single most important factor in determining whether or not a story *works*. Following are six considerations about POV that may help you make the right choices for your story.

Select the Correct Number of POVs

It's often tempting to share *everything* that *every character* is thinking. But few stories (not to mention readers) can handle a plot that includes twenty POVs. Less is very often more. Some of the most powerful novels are those that focus on a single POV. Additional

POVs may alert your reader to additional details, but they can also water down the force of the main POV. It's important to realize readers don't need (or even appreciate) knowing every little detail. Sometimes what you don't say is more powerful than what you do. Plus, the fewer POVs you have, the less risk you run of either boring or confusing the reader. There's no writing law that gives a limit to POV characters, but here are a few tips for figuring out how many are too many.

- POV usually indicates an important character, since it gives readers an intimate look into the character's mind.

- Using more than one POV allows readers to see things through more than one character's mind.

- The more POV characters you have, the more you're forcing your readers to spread out both their attention and their loyalty.

- Multiple POVs can fragment your story and weaken its focus.

Consider carefully every time you decide to introduce a new POV. Does this new POV add something vital to the story—or could the scenes be reworked into an existing POV character's viewpoint?

Choose the POV of the Character With the Most at Stake

Toward the end of *Dreamlander*, I needed to write a tense scene in which the hero reveals some tragic news to his allies. I struggled with the scene for several days, writing and rewriting from my hero's POV. Then, suddenly, it struck me: I was writing from the wrong POV. My hero was *not* the character with the most to lose in this scene. Because I had already dramatized his discovery of the tragedy in a previous scene and because he had already come to grips with it, his POV in this scene provided nothing new. In fact, all my attempts to inject drama felt repetitious in light of the earlier scenes. With that in mind, I looked around for the character who would be most affected by the news, and my scene took flight. All the tension, drama, and angst I had been searching for immediately came to the forefront when I switched to a character whose emotions were at a keener pitch.

Choose the POV of the Character With the Most Interesting Voice

The character you choose as your main POV will influence the entire tone of the novel. It's often wise to look beyond the obvious choice of POV and see what your other characters have to offer. Several years ago, I nearly burnt myself out writing and rewriting the first fifty pages of a World War II drama that refused to cooperate. I had my plot mapped out, I was in love with my characters, and I knew exactly the tone I was striving for. But I couldn't quite achieve it. My innocent, naïve, and sweet-tempered heroine just didn't have the chops to carry the narrative. After setting the manuscript aside for several months, I realized I had been telling the wrong story all along. I switched POVs to the snarky, cynical viewpoint of an American reporter, who had been a minor character up to that point, and the narrative took off (although the story stalled out again later, perhaps permanently, for different reasons).

Play Around With Voice and Tense

Once you've mastered the basics of POV (particularly learning how to recognize and avoid the universal beginner's habit of "head hopping"), POV becomes an exciting playground, full of all kinds of possibilities. Many writers find a niche in one voice or another and stay there. But don't be afraid to play around. My first eight novels were all written in third-person past tense. Allowing myself to explore different viewpoints and tenses in my most recent novel stretched my writing skills in ways I never imagined and produced a much stronger story as a result.

STRUCTURING YOUR STORY

It's beyond the scope of this book to discuss story structure in detail (we'll save that for a book on *plotting*), but let's take a look at a quick checklist of the structural possibilities for the beginning, middle, and end of your story. Keep in mind your outline doesn't need to contain *all* of these elements. Consider the following, but always listen to the needs of your story.

Beginning

- Begin with the main character (the MC), so readers immediately understand who this story is about.

- Show readers the MC's "normal world." This is the life he has chosen to live, the life in which he's reasonably comfortable or at least complacent.

- Show readers the MC in a "characteristic moment." Try to create a scene that exhibits both the MC's prominent personality trait and an activity that will feature later in the story.

- Begin with movement. From the first moment readers see him, the MC should be in action. No sitting around, staring at the scenery.

- Give readers a reason to care about or empathize with the MC. Is he brave, smart, tough, kind, funny? Show readers this is a character they're going to enjoy spending time with.

- Give the MC a desire and a goal. What does he want in life? What does he believe he must accomplish in order to achieve that desire?

- Create an inciting event that forever changes the MC's status quo. Rock the character's world in a way he didn't see coming. Perhaps his family is murdered. Perhaps he is caught cheating on an important test. Or perhaps he unexpectedly time travels twenty years into the future.

- Force the MC to react to the inciting event. The inciting event doesn't matter until the protagonist reacts to it. *How* he chooses to react will set the tone for the story to follow.

Middle

- Trap the MC in a spiral of events outside of his control. Set the line of dominoes in motion.

• Force the MC's original goal out of his reach. He can still see it and certainly still wants it, but he can't reach it.

• Give the MC new goals. The MC's primary goal shifts to the background as he struggles to stay afloat with all the complications coming his way.

• Cause the MC to make a decision that shifts him from reacting to the antagonist into full-blown attack mode. He's tired of just sitting there and taking it. Now he's got a plan and he's ready to fight back.

Ending

• Bring the MC to a new understanding of himself (particularly his fatal flaw) and how he needs to become someone better to defeat his antagonist. The most powerful stories are those in which the MC can't obtain physical victory without also obtaining a mental and moral victory within himself.

• Stretch your MC's resolve (physically, mentally, and morally) to the breaking point. Battles should never be easily won. Keep readers in doubt of the hero's ability to triumph.

• Revive the MC at the last moment. Just as the reader thinks the MC is about to cave under the pressure, let him bounce back.

• Transform the MC into a hero. He should dig down deep inside, find a spark of extraordinariness, and rise to the challenge.

• Force the MC to respond in a unique way. How can he respond to the climactic forces in a way distinctive to his personality?

• Show the MC defeating the opponent. Or not, depending on your story. But, either way, the battle between your hero and the antagonist should come to a definitive conclusion.

• Let the MC reach his goals. Assuming your story is one in

which the hero triumphs, the MC will be able to move past the now-defeated antagonist to achieve the goals that have eluded him throughout the story. Perhaps he finds peace in the aftermath of his family's deaths. Perhaps, now having repented of cheating, he studies for the test, retakes it, and gets that A he needs. Perhaps he comes to grips with his new time-traveling power and uses it to improve his ability to live in the present.

- End with a memorable line. Readers will remember the ending more than any other part of your story, so make it unforgettable!

THREE FUNDAMENTAL ELEMENTS OF STORY

Once your beginning, middle, and ending form a skeleton strong enough to hold your story upright, it's time to begin adding muscle and flesh, in the form of relationships, action, and humor. Take a gander at your bookshelf, maybe even pull a couple titles, and see if you can pick out these common threads. I grabbed three books off my shelves: *The Long Roll* by Mary Johnston, *H.M.S. Surprise* by Patrick O'Brian, and *Firebird* by Kathy Tyers. This is a pretty random selection that contains a little of everything: authors of both genders, two semi-classics, publication dates ranging from 1911 to 1999, and genres as varied as historical and science fiction. But the three things we're guaranteed to find in common are—you guessed it—relationships, action, and humor.

Humor

Let's begin with humor, since it's arguably the least important in our triad of essentials. Although I say least, that certainly doesn't negate its importance. Humor not only possesses the power to entertain the reader and endear him to the characters, it is also essential in balancing the darker elements in serious fictional situations. In "A Letter to a Young Talented Writer," playwright and short story author William Saroyan advised us to "...remember that in the midst of that which is most tragic, there is always the comic...."[26]

Two of my selected books—*The Long Roll* and *Firebird*—are dark, wrenching stories. But their moments of lightheartedness bring a powerful contrast. Patrick O'Brian, a master of irony and understatement, wrote of war and the nature of man, but his incisive wit and nonchalant humor lifted his stories above the sordidness of life and elevated them to philosophical brilliance.

Action

Certainly, many stories—lauded classics, even—have been written in which little to no visible action takes place on the page. But, as we've already discussed, the best stories, the enduring stories, are *always* about conflict. And conflict translates into action. Whether it's the stunning space battles in the work of Orson Scott Card or the subtle machinations and maneuverings of George Eliot's society set, action constitutes the cogs inside the clockwork of a story. Action moves the story forward, inexorably, across the thematic arc to an inevitable conclusion.

The Long Roll, the first installment in Mary Johnston's epic American Civil War duology, is ultimately a biography of the conflict itself, with characters often taking a backseat to the terrifying scope of a national war. In crisp prose, Johnston hypnotizes the reader with the desperate ebb and flow of battle, the surge of individual conflict, and the heat of dreams bleeding away on a churned-up battlefield. More even than in most novels, action *is* Johnston's story, and she drives the conflict home with staggering force.

Relationships

If stories are a reflection of the human experience, and if the human experience boils down to the interaction between people, we should find relationships at the heart of all fiction. Whether it's the romantic connection between a man and a woman (Jane Austen's *Pride & Prejudice*, Emily Brontë's *Wuthering Heights*), varying familial relationships (Louisa May Alcott's *Little Women*, Fyodor Dostoyevsky's *The Adolescent*), or the ever-evolving status of friendship (Sir Arthur Conan Doyle's Sherlock Holmes stories, Charles Dickens's *The Posthumous Papers of the Pickwick Club*), relationships, or occasionally the lamented lack thereof, form the basis of every story.

In her Firebird trilogy, Kathy Tyers follows the threads of several relationships, including the courtship and marriage of Brennan Caldwell and Firebird Angelo and the strained and even violent relations between Firebird and her estranged family. Through the contrast in these relationships and through the anguish of loss found in powerful personal connections, Tyers is able to weave a story of both deep heartbreak and deeper victory.

The amount to which each of these three elements is found in any given book will vary, of course. Some books are able to bring humor to the foreground, others push relationships to the back burner to indulge the action. But, ultimately, these three things are what keep readers turning those pages. These are the elements that inevitably surface in the books that become our personal favorites, and they are elements we must incorporate as we structure our dramatic outlines.

STRENGTHEN YOUR STORY WITH PROPER FRAMING

Framing is a useful, but too often overlooked, technique that gives your story cohesion and directs readers' loyalties and attention. Frames bookend a story with definitive opening scenes that introduce readers to pertinent characters, settings, and themes, and closing scenes that bring the story to a resonant full circle. Consider some of these examples from popular movies:

- *Peter Pan,* **directed by P.J. Hogan (2003):** This adaptation of J.M. Barrie's play and book offers an especially obvious example of framing, since it was able to use the same opening shot, with a slight variation, as its closing scene. The movie opens with a line of text on the screen ("All children grow up… except one"), which, when repeated by the narrator at the film's end, not only underlines the theme, but also brings the story to a beautiful full circle.

- *The Patriot,* **directed by Roland Emmerich (2000):** The movie begins and ends with the South Carolinian farm that symbolizes everything the characters fought and, in some instances, died for during the American War for Independence. It opens with an idyllic look at the peaceful farm life (the character's "normal world"), which is soon to be destroyed by the imminent war. It ends, after the war, when the surviving characters return to rebuild the farm, which, again, is symbolic of the reconstruction the entire nation was going through.

• *Forever Young*, **directed by Steve Miner (1992):** The framing here is subtler, in that both the beginning and, particularly, the closing scenes are directly inherent to the plot— and the story is all the stronger for it. The opening shot features an early version of the B-25 airplane careening through the skies, while test pilot Daniel McCormick gleefully struggles to keep it under control. The B-25 reappears throughout the movie as a symbol of what the main character loses by sleeping through fifty years of his life, and, in the end, as the key factor in the gambit to reunite the rapidly aging character with his lost love. The movie that opened with the plane plummeting out of the sky closes with a scene of the plane landing in a sunset-backed field.

• *White Christmas*, **directed by Michael Curtiz (1954):** This holiday classic features a beautiful use of framing that incorporates both plot and theme. It opens behind the battle lines in World War II, with the main characters hosting a revue for the men, both in celebration of Christmas and as a farewell to their beloved general. The finale, which takes place several years later, brings the story full circle, ending with another revue on Christmas Eve, in honor of the now-retired general.

A solid frame grounds your story, neatly foreshadows things to come, and leaves readers with a tidy ending that resonates. Paying attention to framing in the outlining stages will not only save you time in the long run, it will also give you opportunities to grow symbols and recurrent settings and themes organically from your plot.

THE DOMINO EFFECT: MAKE EVERY SCENE MATTER

What is it that makes a novel a novel and not just a collection of short stories? The difference is that a novel is a cohesive whole, in which every scene is so integrally related that to remove one scene would throw the whole story out of whack. Novels are like an elaborate domino pattern—you know the type, the complicated curlicues and whorls that cover hundreds of square feet and require hours upon hours to construct. When every domino is in place, all you have to do is flick that first one, and they all fall in perfect synchronicity. But if even one domino is out of place, the whole pattern screeches to a silent halt.

Imagine every scene in your novel is a domino in the grand pattern of your story. If the reader is going to be able to topple the pattern and see every domino fall, the author has to design his scenes so each one directly influences those that follow. Every scene has to *matter*. If you write a scene that fails to influence the scenes that follow—if you could delete it from the story without its making a whit of difference to the plot—then you either need to delete it or come up with a way to *make* it matter.

In *The Flight of the Falcon*, one of Daphne du Maurier's little-known works, she exhibits her mastery of the domino effect. Every scene in her story, no matter how seemingly innocuous or disconnected from the main plot, has a purpose. She never wastes an opportunity. Walk-on characters, casual dialogue, random bits of description—they all tie into the web she's weaving around her readers. This is exemplified in a scene late in the book in which the main character, during a ramble on the beach, stops to talk to a nun who is minding several children. Their conversation is the noncommittal, relatively impersonal exchange we would expect from two strangers. A few pages later, the nun leaves the scene, her part in the book complete.

At first glance, the nun's scene might appear to be a useless intrusion into the plot, a filler while the main character awaits his appointment, or an attempt by the author to introduce some local color into the description. But as the story enters the climax, we realize du Maurier used this scene to introduce crucial information that caused it to be a turning point for the main character. This simple "filler" became a domino that influenced all the scenes to come. If we can follow her example in mastering this technique, we will streamline our writing so our stories can power ahead at full steam, unimpeded by dead weight.

Reverse Outlining

When you think of outlines, you generally think about organization, right? The whole point of outlining, versus the seat-of-the-pants method, is to give the writer a road map, a set of guidelines, a plan. An outline should be simple, streamlined, and linear. An outline should put things in order. So you're probably going to think I'm crazy when I tell you one of the most effective ways to make certain every scene matters is to outline *backwards*.

During the outlining process, we have to create a plausible series of events, a chain reaction that will cause each scene to domino into the one following. But linking scenes isn't always easy to do, if you don't know what it's supposed to be linking *to*. As any mystery writer can tell you, you can't set the clues up perfectly until you know whodunit. Often, it's easier and more productive to start with the *last* scene in a series and work your way backwards.

For example, in my outline of a historical story, I knew one of my POV characters was going to be injured so badly he would be unable to communicate with another character for almost a month. However, I didn't yet know how or why he was injured. I could work my way toward this point in a logical, linear fashion, starting at the last known scene (a dinner party), and building one scene upon another, until I reached my next known point (the injury). But because my chain of events was based on what was already behind me (the dinner party), more than what was away off in the future (the injury), my attempts to bridge the two were less than cohesive.

Had I outlined these scenes in a linear fashion, squeezing in the injury might have become a gymnastic effort instead of a natural flowing of plot. Plus, the fact that I had no idea what was supposed to happen between the dinner party and the injury meant I was likely to invent random and inconsequential events to fill the space.

My solution?

You got it: work backwards.

Starting at the end of the plot progression—the injury—I began asking questions that would help me discover the plot development immediately preceding. How was the character hurt? Where was he hurt? Why did the bad guys choose to do this to him? Why was he only injured, instead of killed? How is he going to escape? Following is a portion of my backwards outline:

> After Bruce leaves Wendy at the party, I know he's going to be so seriously injured that he goes incommunicado for a month. Somehow the party has to lead into his injury. What's the injury going to be? Is he shot, knifed, what? That might depend on the general circumstances. Why is he shot/knifed? Where? Etc.
>
> Presumably, he's hurt as a result of his investigation into Charles's wrongdoings. Bruce is making enough of a nuisance of himself that Charles wants him out of the way. Is Bruce about to break the case? Maybe he takes his evidence to the higher authorities, and the high authority—partially from apathy and corruption, partly as a result of Charles's dissembling—fails to do anything. So, as usual, Bruce decides to take matters into his own hands. At the very least, he wants to free Wendy from Charles's blackmailing. So, as a last ditch effort, he goes to Charles himself and makes demands. Charles would probably just laugh at him at first, and then when Bruce inevitably started throwing his weight around, Charles might give in—only to send his lackeys after Bruce to waylay him.
>
> So the lackeys get Bruce off someplace alone and mess him up pretty severely. Charles would have no reason to keep him alive, so the question now is how Bruce avoids being killed. Maybe his partner Isaacs has something to do with that?
>
> What if we had some kind of car chase/crash—just to give us some variation from the shoot-'em-up scenes to come? So Bruce is driving home from Charles's house, and the bad guys

run him off the road. Why don't they kill him after they crash his car?

I suppose Isaacs could show up and shoot them. But that's pretty messy—not very conducive to a silent disappearance. Maybe Bruce has some kind of spectacular crash, and the bad guys just leave him for dead.

So how does this help us build scenes up from where I left off? Well, now I know that Bruce gathers enough information to convict—but not hang—Charles. Also, something—some ticking time bomb that climaxes at the dinner party—forces him to confront Charles in order to free Wendy.

Once I knew these things, I knew how I needed to set the scene up, and once I knew how to set the scene up, I knew what to put in the previous slot in the outline. Eventually, I was able to work myself all the way back to the dinner party. *Voilà!* I now had a complete sequence of events, all of which were cohesive, linear, and logical enough to make my story tight and intense.

Facing the wide unknown of a story is scary, and putting one foot in front of the other, when you're unsure of the terrain, can be overwhelming. But when you can work your way backwards from a known point, finding your way becomes as simple as filling in the blanks. The result is a story that falls into order like a row of expertly placed dominoes.

Chapter Nine Checklist

- ☑ Write your extended outline, scene by scene, numbering each new section.
- ☑ Decide how to make this story your "perfect novel."
- ☑ Determine your audience demographic.
- ☑ Select which POV(s) and tense you will write from.
- ☑ Double-check the structure of your beginning, middle, and ending.
- ☑ Verify that your story contains humor, action, and relationships.

☑ Frame your story with a cohesive and resonant beginning and ending that complement and strengthen each other.

☑ Set your scenes up like a row of dominos, each one influencing those that follow.

☑ Eliminate any unnecessary scenes.

☑ Outline backwards when you're unsure how to get from Point A to Point B.

ASKING THE AUTHORS

Bio: The author of the memoir *Freedom's Just Another Word*, Dan L. Hays hosts the inspirational podcast *Minute to Freedom* and the radio program *Dialogue With Dignity* and writes the blog *Thoughts Along the Road to Healing*. Visit him at danlhays.com.

Can you describe your outlining process?

An outline is analogous to reading a map before a road trip. I find my starting point, then pick out the best route to where I'm headed. First, I determine where the story begins. I also have an approximate idea where the story ends. I say approximate because the story may shift as I write it. Having a starting and ending point gives me a timeline. For my first novel, that timeline was four months. For the current memoir I'm writing, the timeline is thirty years. The longer timeline has made it essential to have a solid outline and idea of where the story is going. I periodically check the road map along the way, to make sure I'm still on the right path.

What is the greatest benefit of outlining?

When I begin to write that first chapter, I have the road map in the back of my mind, which helps enormously in the first draft. If I've wandered off course, I can more readily sense it and pull back from the extraneous direction. In my first memoir, I had numerous threads I left out of the manuscript, because they weren't part of the story I was trying to tell. I wanted to focus on the interaction between me and my father and how his death impacted me. The outline helped me stay on that path.

What is the biggest pitfall of outlining?

Serving the outline, rather than using it as a tool to serve me. Once I lay out the basic structure of the book, I don't want to adhere rigidly to the outline to the detriment of the story. I have to allow the creative component to invest my process, to help me learn the true story along the way.

DAN L. HAYS

Sometimes unexpected moments happen, and I want to be free to capture them.

I think the best way to avoid becoming too rigid in outlining is to allow for adjustments along the way. A canoe doesn't go across the lake in a straight line. As the rower paddles on one side or the other, the canoe moves slightly back and forth across the intended path. I think allowing the outline to work that same way gives it the maximum benefit without hindering the creative process.

Do you recommend "pantsing" for certain situations and outlining for others?

If you don't know where you're going, you won't know where you'll end up. For some people "pantsing" might work well, but it just doesn't fit for me. Within a shorter segment, such as a chapter, I will work without an outline, writing the scenes as they unfold. However, I do have an outline for the larger work, so the scenes have already in a sense been outlined. For a short piece—such as a blog post or a short article—I'm a lot more likely to "pants." I am a storyteller by nature; even my blog posts tend toward a story structure.

What's the most important contributing factor to a successful outlining experience?

An outline has to have the fluidity to shift according to the needs of the story. I usually take a long time to write a novel or a memoir—typically several years. If I wasn't working within a structure, I would get lost and veer far off course. My writing process begins by flying high above the story and laying out the nature of the forest—the outline does that for me. Then I dip down and describe the trees and the path through the forest from a very close perspective. Without the road map, I might take the wrong path and not even know it. I can tell some very entertaining stories that sound really wonderful, but don't fit the story I'm currently trying to tell.

But, as I walk through the forest, describing the process and my journey, I have to have the flexibility to encounter the unexpected and embrace it. If my outline is Roman Numeral I, A & B, I have to allow for the possibility that there is a C that needs to be included, which I might not realize until I get to that point.

"I've found that people who outline a lot spend more time up front planning. People who discover their story by writing it spend more time at the end revising. It tends to even out."
—*Brandon Sanderson*[27]

10

THE ABBREVIATED OUTLINE: DRAWING YOUR ROAD MAP

ONCE YOU'VE FINISHED outlining your plot, it's time to condense the pertinent info into an Abbreviated Outline. The Abbreviated Outline will keep you from having to read your entire Extended Outline every time you sit down to write. It will provide you an at-a-glance road map that highlights all the important stops along the way to your destination. This is the guide you'll refer to while writing your official first draft. Of course, if you want to, you can skip this step and use your Extended Outline while writing. But I choose to summarize my notes and type them up on the computer for several reasons:

> • **It cuts out the rambling.** Because the Extended Outline offers us the opportunity to solve problems, explore dead ends, and sort through hundreds of ideas in search of the dozen or so worth keeping, it's inevitably full of digression and repetition. Much of the word count in my Extended Outline isn't something I need to re-read to help myself understand the story. I don't necessarily need to save the information about *how* I reached a decision; in writing my first draft, I only need to know what that decision *is*.

- **Makes it legible.** Do we really need to talk about my handwriting again? Typing my notes into the computer means saving myself from repeatedly having to decipher my handwriting. While transcribing, I'll also fix my spelling, punctuation, and grammar—and generally streamline my thoughts to make them intelligible.

- **Distills the pertinent points.** An Abbreviated Outline allows me to see the prominent plot points at a glance. A quick scroll down the screen, and I've seen my entire story arc in a few seconds. Were I to leave my notes within the welter of my handwritten Extended Outline, I would have to read paragraphs upon paragraphs per scene.

- **Saves time.** Transcribing my notes can take several weeks, but it saves time in the long run. Instead of having to flip through two or three notebooks, wading through all the extraneous chatter while trying to remember where I might have written a particular idea, I can use the Find feature on my computer to zip right to the pertinent info.

In days of yore, I used to type the Abbreviated Outline in Word and print a copy for easy reference. But ever since I discovered the superior organizational features of the software program yWriter, I've used it to store and organize my Abbreviated Outline notes. (You can find information about downloading and using yWriter in Chapter Two.)

Because I went through my Extended Outline notes at the end of each outlining session and used my blue highlighter to mark the bits I wanted to keep, I've saved myself the trouble of having to reread the entirety of my notes. Instead, all I have to do is look for the blue bits and type them up under the appropriate scene and chapter headings.

Your Abbreviated Outline, in its simplest form, might look something like mine from *Behold the Dawn*:

1. Gethin confronts Annan in Italy, and Annan follows him to the Crusade.

2. Roderic hires Annan to kill Matthias, Gethin, and William and kidnap Mairead; Annan agrees only to kill Matthias.

3. Roderic is unsure how to take the news of Annan's "accepting" the job.

4. Annan is injured in the siege of Acre and taken prisoner.

5. He is nursed by Mairead, the wife of his one-time mentor, Lord William, who is dying.

6. Richard slaughters the Saracen prisoners.

7. William requests Annan marry Mairead and protect her.

8. Annan and Mairead escape with Gethin's aid.

9. Roderic decides to send Hugh and Warin to kill Annan and Mairead.

If you prefer, your Abbreviated Outline can include more information than just these one-sentence summaries. I used more in-depth scene descriptions in *Dreamlander*, as demonstrated by these excerpts from the middle of the outline:

51. Allara decides to visit the Garowai because she can feel something's not right. Chris gives a recruiting speech to the citizens of Glen Arden. Among those who join up to fight are Orrick and Markham. (I *probably* don't need to go into great detail with this. Recruiting speeches are pretty boring. Open this chapter in Allara's POV and just more or less make the comment that Chris gained some new recruits.)

Allara prepares to ride out of the city at the same time as Chris and his men. She happens to stop next to Chris's sisters. They exchange a few comments about Chris, highlighting Allara's confusion of emotions after the balcony scene the night before. Allara is finding herself more and more drawn to Chris. Her former antipathy for him has all but faded. Now, she is truly growing to respect him. He is proving himself a valiant and honorable person. She feels safer around him, stronger. He makes her want to believe. For the first time in her life, she's met someone who is actually capable of sharing her great burden—and helping her bear it. She is less a Searcher around him—and more a... woman. She's met few men capable of being bigger than her—stronger—wiser—braver. She's used to being the responsible one, the strong one. But with him, she doesn't have to pull him up—she's learning to just lean into his strength. For the first time in a long time, she has a reason to believe, and Chris Redston is that reason.

Anyhow, as Allara's conversation with the Bowen ladies winds down, Chris looks up and catches her eye and smiles. They should exchange a few words. Then they part ways.

52. Chris gets stuck in a skirmish on the army's flank, with Pitch somehow at the center of things. Pitch escaped Mactalde and made it across the river to tell Chris Orias is in trouble. Pitch may disapprove of some of Orias's actions of late, but he loves Orias too much to ever betray him. Pitch knows where Mactalde has placed an artillery battlement, so Chris and Co. go off to destroy that.

53. Allara rides off to have her talk with the Garowai. Since we're jumping from the tense scene of skirmishing over an artillery battlement to this, the tension in the conversation needs to be tight. Allara starts out asking for the Garowai to make an appearance at Glen Arden to help quell the Nateros sentiments—which she is naturally pretty tense about. And from there (with a little help from Quinnon), the conversation switches to Chris. Allara asks again why the Garowai never told her another Gifted was coming, and Quinnon interjects some pretty pointed remarks, prodding the Garowai for info about Chris.

ORGANIZING AND ANALYZING YOUR SCENES

Transferring your scenes into your Abbreviated Outline gives you your first opportunity to analyze your raw material, cut what doesn't work, and strengthen what does. Be on the watch for unnecessary scenes that can be deleted or combined with one or more equally floppy scenes. Could your character get the phone call about her mother's death while she's en route to her hearing? Although you could certainly cut and paste and combine scenes after writing the first draft, it's so much easier to make these adjustments in the outline.

Consider each scene's importance and effectiveness. Make note of scenes that can be deleted, scenes that can be combined, and scenes that are weak. This goes for characters and settings as well. Can you streamline your cast by combining two or more minor characters? The fewer characters you have, the more focused your story will be and the fewer loose ends you'll have to tie up at the end. However, as important as it is to keep streamlining techniques in mind, don't be afraid to let your story tell itself the way it *needs* to be told.

DIVIDING YOUR STORY INTO CHAPTERS AND SCENES

Although you may choose (as I do) not to break your book into chapters until after the first draft is finished, the Abbreviated Outline is the time to start looking for likely places for chapter and scene breaks. Often, your story will naturally break at appropriately dramatic moments. Be on the hunt for ways you can incorporate strong scene endings into your outline.

Keep Readers Reading

Scene breaks are do-or-die territory for novelists. You may be spinning a grand ol' tale, full of fascinating characters, but if your chapter and scene endings leave readers no reason to turn the page and find out what happens next, all your hard work on the other aspects of your story will be wasted. Not every scene needs to end with a cliffhanger, but they do need to encompass a question powerful enough to make the reader crazy to know the answer.

This is no easy task, in large part because not every scene is going to feature huge revelations and startling questions. How do you mine your story for the tension and conflict that will translate into the most powerful question a reader can ask: *What's gonna happen next?* Following are eleven suggestions for turning your blasé endings into killer chapter breaks:

1. Promise of conflict.
Example: The hero has just been challenged to a duel.
Inherent Question: Will he survive?

2. A secret kept.
Example: The hero's partner hides a letter.
Inherent Question: What's in the confounded letter?

3. A major decision or vow.
Example: The hero swears to avenge his wife's murder.
Inherent Question: How will he go about it? Will he succeed?

4. An announcement of a shocking event.
Example: The hero's father dies.
Inherent Question: How did he die? How is the hero going to react?

5. A moment of high emotion.
Example: The hero is enraged by the promotion of an incompetent coworker.
Inherent Question: How will the hero express his anger? Will he experience repercussions?

6. A reversal or surprise that turns the story upside down.
Example: The heroine discovers her long-dead mother isn't dead at all.
Inherent Question: Where has the mother been all this time? How is the heroine going to adjust to this new paradigm?

7. A new idea.
Example: The hero comes up with a new scheme for defeating the bad guy.
Inherent Question: Will it work?

8. An unanswered question.

Example: "You're not who you said you were, are you?"

Inherent Question: Is he who he said he was? If not, who is he? And why did he lie about his identity?

9. A mysterious line of dialogue.

Example: "You'll find your answers on the Northside Bridge, midnight. Come alone."

Inherent Question: What are the answers? Why the Northside Bridge? Why midnight? Why alone?

10. A portentous metaphor.

Example: A solar eclipse over a battlefield.

Inherent Question: Is this an indication of tragedy to come?

11. A turning point.

Example: The heroine is shipped off to an orphanage.

Inherent Question: What will happen in her new life? How will she adapt?

Use a wide variety of breaks to keep your readers guessing. It's possible—and even preferable—to use all of these examples in one story. Ending every scene with a cliffhanger can become monotonous, so don't feel as if the tension has to be ratcheted to the breaking point at the end of every scene. Make sure your readers are left with a question—a reason to find out more—and, before they know it, they'll have read your entire book in one sitting.

Control Pacing

You're probably familiar with the common wisdom that writing shorter sentences during action scenes contributes to a sense of tension and speed. If you want a scene to move quickly, think short. If you want it to move leisurely, lengthen the rhythm of your writing. The same holds just as true for scene and chapter length.

Ruth Downie's boisterous, tongue-in-cheek Gaius Petreius Ruso series, features extremely short chapters. Some are barely longer than a page. Due in no small part to this simple trick, her historical mysteries rush along at a madcap pace that perfectly suits her humorous tone and her hapless main character. In contrast to the fifty-plus chapters in Downie's books, the similarly sized books in Patrick O'Brian's lauded Aubrey/Maturin series rarely feature more than ten chapters. His decision to use chapters of fifty or more pages fits nicely within his series' historical tone and lends gravitas to his characters' seafaring adventures during the Napoleonic War.

Downie's and O'Brian's respective decisions on scene and chapter length effortlessly contribute to the fast-paced, modern tone of the one and the historic, slightly detached perspective of the other. Consider the needs of your story and apply this simple trick of pacing to control your overall goal of tone and energy. It's unlikely you'll be able to tell how long your scenes and chapters will turn out, just from your outline notes, but now is a good time to start planning your pacing, so you can order your scenes accordingly when you start writing.

Cut the Fat

The task of trimming fat is much easier in an outline of a few hundred words than it is in a manuscript of a hundred thousand, and you'll probably find one of your most flagrant areas of fat accumulation is in scene transitions that recount characters moving between settings. In his breakout fantasy *Elantris*, Brandon Sanderson shows us how to trim these pointless filler bits by utilizing one of our most useful and invisible tools: the scene break.

Although Sanderson's book is no lightweight—it weighs in at almost 700 pages—he does a good job cutting out the boring fat that could easily have doubled his page count. He uses scene breaks not only in the obvious places to indicate changes of POV or setting, but also to cut even seemingly innocuous segments, such as, in one instance, his antagonist climbing a lengthy flight of stairs. The result Sanderson produces not only trims the fat from his story, it also contributes to a sense of speed in his pacing. He could easily have written a short sentence that would have brushed over the antagonist's climb up the stairs, but thanks to the scene break, he indicates the passage of time to the reader in a tight, snappy fashion that keeps his story rolling right along.

As you transcribe your outline, into Word, yWriter, or your word processor of choice, pay attention to the construction and flow of your scenes. Make note of places where you can use a scene or chapter break to create the suspense and rhythm you're looking for.

Chapter Ten Checklist

- ☑ Transcribe pertinent notes from your Extended Outline into your word processor of choice.
- ☑ Weigh each scene's effectiveness, strengthen those that are weak, and eliminate those that are unnecessary.
- ☑ Divide your story into scenes and chapters at appropriately dramatic intervals.

ASKING THE AUTHORS

Bio: The author of *The Writer's Guide to Psychology* (Quill Driver), Carolyn Kaufman has a doctorate in clinical psychology and uses it to teach college in the American Midwest. She also runs the *Archetype Writing: Psychology for Fiction Writers* website. Visit her at archetypewriting.com.

Can you describe your outlining process?

I write major plot points on different index cards (I prefer the kind without lines) and think of them as stepping stones. The cards are nice because you can start with just an inkling of an idea and add as you go. If I come up with something major that falls in between two cards, it's easy to add a card. I can also discard and rearrange cards as necessary.

What is the greatest benefit of outlining?

As I said, I think of the cards as stepping stones. They help ground me and give me a place to put my proverbial feet as I work my way through the story. I'm less likely to end up feeling lost or confused about what to write when I sit down with the file each day. (I hate feeling lost and confused. I open the file, stare at it, click around in it, read a bit here and there, and wonder what the heck to write. Not productive at all.)

A quirk of mine is that I need to write the story in chronological order. I know a lot of people write scenes out of order, but that doesn't work for me. The cards give me a place to write down the ideas for future scenes without actually writing the scenes. That way I don't lose or forget material ahead of me as I work in my current place in the manuscript.

What is the biggest pitfall of outlining?

When you've done the work to outline a path through a story, it can be hard to go a different direction, even if you realize you need to as you work. Some of my very best plot points have come from characters doing unexpected things. For example, one key character who was definitely not supposed

CAROLYN KAUFMAN

to die did just that. I did everything I could to get her up again, but she just... died on me. It ended up making the whole second half of the novel better, because it introduced crazy conflict among the other characters. It also created a reason for a second book.

Do you recommend "pantsing" for certain situations and outlining for others?

I have actually written more by the seat of my pants than I have with an outline, but I'm finding it harder to do that as I mature as a writer and recognize the importance of plot, theme, pacing, and so forth. Also, as I've learned to write for publication, I've realized it's very difficult to come back and work as hard as I need to on a project that has little direction when I have other writing (often nonfiction) that *does*. So I go back to liking the flexibility of note cards. They don't lock me into an unfolding story in a rigid way, and they leave me plenty of room to fill in the holes between the cards and write the scenes themselves in a spontaneous way.

What's the most important contributing factor to a successful outlining experience?

Stay flexible and have fun with it. I like the way classic, organized outlines look, but I'm really more of an intuitive person, and I can get trapped by trying to make a traditional outline look nice if I take that approach. That is, I get caught up in the process of making the outline just so, as if I were back in school and doing it for a grade, rather than using it as a tool. So instead of trying to make a true outline, I keep in mind that this is a creative and sometimes messy process, and that it's okay to draw little pictures on my note cards, or add passing thoughts, or color, or whatever will help me capture the ideas I have for that "stepping stone," so I'll remember later what I was thinking.

"The outline is 95 percent of the book. Then I sit down and write, and that's the easy part."
—Jeffery Deaver[28]

11

CONCLUSION: USING YOUR OUTLINE

CONGRATULATIONS! YOU'VE NOW reached the end of the outlining process. After several months of diligent preparation, you're ready to embark on a road trip down the Interstate and the dusty back roads of your story. You've decided on your destination, you've mapped your route, and you've packed your equipment. All that's left is to buckle yourself into your desk chair and rev up your computer. Adventure waits ahead, much of it anticipated—but you can be sure you'll encounter more than a few surprises. You'll probably break down on the side of the road more than once. You'll run into construction work and a detour or two. And you may decide to ditch the map for the occasional afternoon of exploration whenever an intriguing sideroad catches your eye.

It's time to put your completed outline to use. You'll refer to it every day before settling in to write, you'll use it to reference events yet to come in your story, and you'll use it to double-check facts for consistency. The beauty of it all is that when you sit down at your computer and the cursor starts winking at you from the depths of your blank screen, you don't have to panic with the thought that you have *no* idea what to write. All you have to do is open your outline file and find the next turn on your map. Flip your blinker, and you're all set for another day's drive through your story.

For many of us, writing is all about tapping that sense of freedom—the promise that anything could be waiting for us around the next bend in the road. Some writers fear outlining will destroy that freedom by locking them into a set route. But the truth is just the opposite. *Freedom* is knowing you never have to stare down the blinking cursor and the blank page because you don't know what comes next. You're still free to explore all you want, but, at the end of the day, when the detour turns out to be a dead end, you can always return to the marked path you know will lead to your destination. With your route highlighted on the map, you're free to put on your sunglasses, crank up your tunes, and let your hair blow in the wind.

The trick to using your outline to gain maximum productivity is remembering an outline is as fluid as you want it to be. When you reach Chapter Five and realize you're missing a prime opportunity to deepen your heroine's character by showing how she handles a spat with her stepmother, you can change the outline on the spot. Remember: the outline is a guideline, not a law etched in stone.

The outline is the tool of the responsible author who understands that story is as much about structure as it is about inspiration. Melding these twin juggernauts allows us to create a story that flows from our deep inner wells of creativity and pour it into the mold of our outline. We could do this in retrospect; we could dump our messy, wonderful, uncontrolled inspiration into our first draft and edit it into a sensible structure. But by utilizing an outline to decipher, organize, and direct our stories, we can save ourselves both time and effort.

In a world where we have so many stories to write, that's a tool worth taking advantage of.

Happy outlining!

Chapter Eleven Checklist

- ☑ Stock up on coffee and chocolate.
- ☑ Crank up your music.
- ☑ Open your manuscript file on your computer.
- ☑ Kick your cat off the keyboard.
- ☑ Review your outline.
- ☑ Rev your writing engines.
- ☑ Have fun!

Note From the Author: Reviews are gold to authors! If you've enjoyed this book, would you consider rating it and reviewing it on Amazon.com?

ENDNOTES

1. Raymond Benson, "The 007 Way to Write a Thriller," *The Writer*, November 2010, p. 25.

2. Jeff VanderMeer, *Booklife* (San Francisco, CA: Tachyon Publications, 2009) p. 202.

3. Sarah Domet, *90 Days to Your Novel* (Cincinnati, OH: Writer's Digest Books, 2010) p. 15.

4. Orson Scott Card, *How to Write Science Fiction and Fantasy* (Cincinnati, OH: Writer's Digest Books, 1990) p. 29.

5. Simon Wood, "Does Your Plot Thicken?," *Writer's Digest*, January 2004, p. 38.

6. John Truby, *The Anatomy of Story* (New York, NY: Faber and Faber, Inc., 2007) p. 17.

7. VanderMeer, pp. 317-318.

8. Nancy Kress, "A Stitch in Time," *Writer's Digest*, May 2003, p. 13.

9. Robert Olen Butler, Janet Burroway, ed., *From Where You Dream* (New York, NY: Grove Press, 2005) pp. 87-88.

10. Charles Ghigna, "Quotes on Writing" <http://www.charles ghigna.com/quotes.html>.

11. Margaret Atwood, quoted in Kristen D. Godsey, "Unlocking the Door," *Writer's Digest*, April 2004, p. 48.

12. Elizabeth George, *Write Away* (New York, NY: HarperCollins Publishers, Inc., 2004) p. 69.

13. Don Chaon, "The Title Game Exercise," quoted in Bret Anthony Johnson, ed., *Naming the World* (New York, NY: Random House Publishing Group, 2007) pp. 38-39.

14. L.M. Montgomery, *Emily of New Moon* (New York, NY: Harper and Row, Publishers, Inc., 1923) p. 1.

15. V. Joshua Adams, quoted in Zachary Petit, "12 Literary Journals Your Future Agent Is Reading," 12 May 2010 <http://www.writers digest.com/article/12-literary-journals-your-future-agent-is-reading>.

16. Card, *Characters and Viewpoint* (Cincinnati, OH: Writer's Digest Books, 1988) pp. 5-6.

17. Janice Hardy, "Bad Guys Who Aren't the Antagonists," 10 February 2009, <http://blog.janicehardy.com/2010/02/you-got-ta-have-enemies.html>.

18. Pauline Kiernan, "Character Backstory Screenwriting—Make It Power Your Emotional Plot" <http://www.unique-screen writing.com/character-backstory-screenwriting.html>.

19. Ernest Hemingway, *Death in the Afternoon* (New York, NY: Scribner, 1932) p. 154.

20. James Scott Bell, "Structure Secrets," *Writer's Digest*, October 2003, p. 19.

21. William Somerset Maugham, *Mr. Maugham Himself* (New York, NY: Doubleday, 1954).

22. Michael Connelly, quoted in Jeff Ayers, "In the 'lab' with Michael Connelly," *The Writer*, October 2009, p. 20.

23. George, p. 19.

24. Patricia Highsmith, "My rules for writing," *The Writer*, February 2008, p. 22.

25. Scott Edelstein, *100 Things Every Writer Needs to Know* (New York, NY: The Berkeley Publishing Group, 1988) p. 22.

26. William Saroyan, "A Letter to a Young Talented Writer," *The Writer*, September 1938.

27. Brandon Sanderson, "The wotmania Files: Interview with Brandon Sanderson (11/15/2005)" <http://ofblog.blogspot.com/2009/02/wotmania-files-interview-with-brandon.html>.

28. Jeffery Deaver <http://www.brainyquote.com/quotes/quotes/j/jefferydea233808.html>.

INDEX

ABOUT THE AUTHOR

K.M. Weiland is the author of the historical western *A Man Called Outlaw* and the medieval epic *Behold the Dawn*. She enjoys mentoring other authors through her blog *Wordplay: Helping Writers Become Authors* (wordplay-kmweiland.blogspot.com), editing services, and her instructional CD *Conquering Writer's Block and Summoning Inspiration*. She lives in western Nebraska. Visit her website: kmweiland.com.

Also by K.M. Weiland

The sins of a bishop.
The vengeance of a monk.
The secrets of a knight.

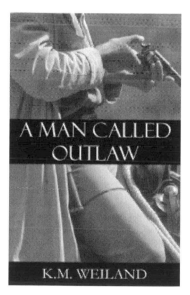

One man stood up unafraid.
One man fell alone.
One man's courage became a legend.

www.kmweiland.com

Position yourself to live an inspired life and send writer's block packing.

In this 60-minute audio presentation, historical and speculative novelist K.M. Weiland shows you how to nurture creativity and put it at your summons, rather than the other way around.

- Build a lifestyle that fosters inspiration
- Say goodbye to destructive guilt over "wasting" time on creative endeavors
- Discover why inspiration isn't so much a feeling as an act of will
- Use your non-writing time to boost your creative energy
- Prevent and combat writer's block
- Instill habits for improving your efficiency and commitment as an author

www.kmweiland.com

1408207R00102

Made in the USA
San Bernardino, CA
15 December 2012